Fruit Loose And Fancy Tree

Timothy J. Lukings

ISBN: 978-1-60791-600-0

DEDICATION

I dedicate my life daily to God, of which this book is a small part. My deepest desire is that this book gives honour to Him and helps fulfil the purpose for which He has called me.

I dedicate this book to my wife, Kris, who continually pours love into my life and gives me constant support in every part of the ministry, including Fruit Loose and Fancy Tree. She truly is a gift from the Lord.

To my children: Jorin, who has been an example of dedication and discipline throughout his life; Holly, who has shown me what love and joy truly is; and Brandon, who is a great example of what it means to be an over-comer.

To my parents, who gave their lives to God when I was a child. This decision changed the life of our family forever and caused them to be a wonderful example of what it means to serve God.

CONTENTS

ACKNOWLEDGMENTS

To my sister-in-law Paula, who donated skill, time and talent to edit this book and to help make it the best it could be.

INTRODUCTION

I have been faced with stark reality. It began with a confrontation by God's Spirit Himself, and has been confirmed by extensive travel to many cities and numerous churches. Although there are exceptions, the church as a whole resembles very little of what God intended for church to look like. I am not speaking of appearance or structure, although arguments may be made in those regards. I am speaking of effectiveness.

Driving into multitudes of cities, towns, and villages I have noticed that some of the most attractive buildings are Christian churches. Steeples adorn the skyline, drawing man's attention to the presence of the church from which it extends. Crosses announce the fundamental belief in the work of Christ by those who attend such a facility. Stained glass windows tell biblical stories. The investments made in such decoration speak to the priority that the community had placed on the place of worship by those who have contributed to its construction. Some are historical sites in their respective locations, opening their doors to visitors who desire to analyze the majesty of their ancient architecture and to learn of their history. Other churches are new and attractive additions to the landscape. Still others are simple structures that highlight a different set of priorities in worship style.

I see people filing into these facilities. Some of them haven't worn anything but jeans and a t-shirt all week. Today they are dressed up to one degree or another. Either they have put on their best jeans and newest t-shirt, or they have gone so far as to put on a suit or a lovely outfit. Their daughters wear little dresses and shiny shoes, and their sons are dressed up as much as little boys are willing to be. Both the building and their congregants adorn the streets.

Looking good! After all, that's what matters isn't it? Admittedly, to some small degree it does matter in western culture. Appearance, however, was not the priority of the one who hung on the cross of Calvary. His cross was pounded together out of coarse lumber and destined to become stained with His own blood. The real cross of Calvary contrasts those beautiful, perfectly symmetrical oak icons that represent our Christianity. Perhaps this contrast is somewhat representative of the way God intended church to be in comparison to the suit-wearing but weakened fruit-bearing Christianity of our day. Christ's church was designed to be on the streets, not by the streets. The real church was intended to point to a risen Christ rather than to the beauty of our worship centres.

The real issue is that the church, to a large degree, looks better on the outside than it ever has. Still, every church I have encountered pales in comparison to the church I read about in the first ten chapters of the book of Acts. It was a church led by unimpressive leaders that were guided and empowered by the Spirit of God. It was a church that grew from one hundred and twenty to over three thousand in a single day, and five thousand shortly thereafter. It was a church that was in the streets of the community proving Christ's continuing existence by their lives, their love, their message, and by the revelation of God's power at work through them.

There is a temptation to fill this book with statistics, but I will resist. You are simply requested to do an honest assessment of the effectiveness of the church in your community, and of your personal walk with God. Wouldn't it be interesting to know what percentage of your city believe in Him? Out of that number it would be good to know what percentage see the church, which is the collective body of Christ, as being attractive enough to make them want to attend. Even more importantly, how many have a personal relationship with God? How many have had a born-again experience? Does the church where you live represent the love of Christ to the population surrounding it? Is the existence of a living Christ revealed through God's power at work through the church in your city or town? How many have come to know Christ there in the last year, months, weeks or days? Let's honestly put today's church on the balance with the baby church we read about in Acts and see how they compare. This book is not about appearance, but about effectiveness.

Let us not forget that we are the church in our communities. This is not a time to point fingers. It is, however, a time for serious introspection. We must consider how much of Christ's love flows through us on a daily basis. We must think about how much of Christ's life and power is revealed through our lives, how many seeds we have planted, how many plants we have watered, and how many souls we have reaped for Christ's kingdom. It is time to assess our success in discipling those younger in the faith than ourselves, leading them to maturity. The ultimate challenge is: Are we fruit bearing Christians? Part of our problem is a limited understanding of what that means, and the process required to become fruit-bearers.

Before there is time for your mind to fully develop the excuses already being formed, let me remind you of this. The same Holy Spirit, who dwelt in Peter, Paul, Stephen, or any others of the great men and women of God, dwells in every believer today. The same power to live and be effective for God is available to you as a believer. Our culture is no more opposed to Christianity than Israel was a few short days after Christ's crucifixion. The same commission and responsibility given to the early believers is the same for the church today. God has not changed. His power has not diminished. His ability to minister through His body has not lessened in any way. His expectations of us as His body are the same. It is we that have changed. Until we admit it, we will do nothing about it.

I see in the Scripture that ineffective Christianity is not acceptable in the mind of Christ. Listen to the words of our Saviour as recorded in the gospel of John: "I am the true grapevine, and my Father is the gardener. He cuts off every branch of mine that doesn't produce fruit, and he prunes the branches that do bear fruit so they will produce even more. You have already been pruned and purified by the message I have given you. Remain in me, and I will remain in you. For a branch cannot produce fruit if it is severed from the vine, and you cannot be fruitful unless you remain in me. "Yes, I am the vine; you are the branches. Those who remain in me, and I in them, will produce much fruit. For apart from me you can do nothing. 6 Anyone who does not remain in me is thrown away like a useless branch and withers. Such branches are gathered into a pile to be burned. But if you remain in me and my words remain in you, you may ask for anything you want, and it will be granted! When you produce much fruit, you are my true disciples. This brings great glory to my Father." (John 15:1-8, NLT).

The message is clear. If you are in line with the vine, you will bear fruit. If you are not bearing fruit, it would indicate that you have been disconnected and are in danger of eternal punishment. These words sound harsh, and if they were mine alone, I would not expect you to listen. However, they are the words of Christ. We had better listen!

The ideals established in this book are high. Like Paul, I make this declaration: "I don't mean to say that I have already achieved these things or that I have already reached perfection. But I press on to possess that perfection for which Christ Jesus first possessed me." (Philippians 3:12, NLT).

We can no longer settle for what we have known. We must strive for Christ's ideals. We must work to attain the fullness of God's intent for us as individual believers and as a church.

In the autumn of 2,000 I had the privilege of going to Pugwash, a very small town in the province of Nova Scotia, Canada. I was ministering nearby, so I took the opportunity to go. It is the town where my grandmother was raised. As a young boy I often heard her speak of it. Because of the many stories she told of people and places,

I had many romantic images of this maritime town. There is not much there really. The population is small. It is a seaport, which creates a certain peaceful yet glorious character. I saw my mother's aunt, whom I hadn't seen since I was a child. I met my mother's cousin. It was nice, but I was there for another reason. I wanted to feel something. I wanted to stand on the soil where Granny played as a child. I wanted to see the farm where Grandpa worked. They were one and the same. I wanted to look out over the ocean, to which the farm extended, knowing that it was in these waters that my grandmother and grandfather played together. I just wanted to imagine for a few minutes. I did all of that.

My time there was brief, and I wanted something to remind me of my visit. I went to a couple of gift shops, but they were filled with meaningless trinkets made in far off places. In the small town of Pugwash, however, there is a factory where world renowned pewter is manufactured and made into all kinds of decorative items. Pewter is an alloy made of tin, lead and copper. In their retail outlet I found everything imaginable made of pewter, all of it very beautiful. Some were useful items such as a lamp, a candle stick holder, or a picture frame. Others were simply decoration. What I bought, however, was not very decorative, nor did it seem to have purpose. I purchased a blob. With six dollars of my hard earned Canadian money I bought a small, unformed piece of pewter. It looks like a stone, and in it is engraved the word "imagine". That was it. That was what I wanted. It spoke to me in a number of ways.

First, that is what I went to Pugwash to do. I went to imagine some of Granny's memories.

Second, it reminded me of the day when God caused me to begin to imagine the church as He intended for church to be. He challenged me to imagine a church in our day and age as effective as the church I read about in Acts 2-10.

I was also reminded that in the natural the church may appear to be just a blob; a group of different people that come together as one meaningless unit. As a church, we can be that way if we so choose. However, just as the tin, lead, and copper are God made substances blended to make pewter, it reminds me that each part of the church has been created by God. When blended together we form something unique in this world that has the potential of becoming something very beautiful. I have been challenged daily by this imagination stone to realize that the church has all the ingredients to reach the full potential of God's plan for us. We can choose to be a meaningless blob in our community, we can merely decorate our street corners, or we can choose to serve a higher purpose. We can choose to hold the light of Christ up to this world like a well-fashioned lamp or candlestick holder. We can choose to be a frame through which the picture of Christ is revealed.

I trust that this book will cause you to begin to imagine your life, and the church in your community becoming as effective as God intends for you to be, and then take steps to become that. I hope we can begin to imagine being laden with godly fruit and winning our communities for Christ. We fast approach the day of Christ's return. No longer do we have time to be "Fruit Loose, and Fancy Tree".

1 FRUIT SALAD, NO NUTS PLEASE

Real worship is never limited to the corporate gathering. Complete worship is totally directed toward God and eventually flows through our lives in such a way that it bears fruit. There is no doubt that our primary purpose on this earth is to bring glory to God through our worship. The church, however, seems to have a problem with a complete understanding of this vital principle. Oh, there is no problem with our intellectual understanding of this topic. You will readily agree with what I am about to say. Our problem lies in application. We are so often guilty of choosing the enjoyable way, somehow ignoring what we know to be true.

I love church worship. I like to boisterously belt out songs of praise, and I like to solemnly enter those times when the worship music leads to the place when music isn't sufficient. I like that place where I am on my knees or my face before God. The music may still be playing, but I am totally separated from my surroundings. At those times I am alone with Him, conscious of His character and giving myself to Him all over again.

Real worship is never contained within the corporate gathering. Complete worship is totally directed toward God and eventually flows through our lives in such a way that it bears fruit. Time and travel have allowed me the privilege of noticing that different churches are adorned by different expressions of worship. Some are very liturgical, emphasizing decorum and focusing on the majesty of our God. Others delight in His work in their lives and the continuous blessings. Songs of praise bring them to a place of great exuberance and they outwardly express their jubilation through their music, the raising of hands, shouts of joy, and dancing before the Lord. Others have a strong emphasis on the character of God, bringing them to that place of awe of His presence. This worship is often characterized by positions of submission and even periods of absolute silence. These are close, intimate times with God. Few churches seem to have found a balanced diet of majesty, thanksgiving, and intimacy in their worship service. Balance in corporate worship is of the essence, but our understanding of worship cannot stop there.

It is almost staggering that churches with great music, amazingly talented musicians, gifted worship leaders, and a strong emphasis on praise and worship are often not growing churches. Some are. Many of those, however, are drawing Christians from other churches that love great music and enjoy that church's particular flavour. Few are coming to know Christ as their personal Saviour. This huge dilemma emphasizes a strong imbalance in our worship. As important as our corporate worship is to God, He is not so concerned with the nature of our worship service as much as He is concerned with the nature of our daily lives. All forms of worship that don't lead to fruitful Christianity are essentially practices that are self-satisfying rather than true acts of worship.

Real worship is never limited to the corporate gathering. Complete worship is totally directed toward God and eventually flows through our lives in such a way that it bears fruit. Worship is a significant factor in keeping the believer in line with the Vine. According to Jesus, fruitfulness is a natural result of that. The respect for God's majesty, joy of receiving His blessings, awe of His presence, and renewed submission to Him must effect our lives to the point where our lives affect others. The way we relate to those around us, both in and outside of the church, will flow out of our life of worship or lack thereof. I remind you of the words of Christ. "Remain in me, and I will remain in you. For a branch cannot produce fruit if it is severed from the vine, and you cannot be fruitful unless you remain in me. 'Yes, I am the vine; you are the branches. Those who remain in me, and I in them, will produce much fruit. For apart from me you can do nothing.'" (John 15:4-5, NLT).

Fruit Salad

For the purposes of this book, let's pretend that I actually like fruit salad. This illustration is a stretch for me personally, but here goes. Imagine a lovely bowl of fruit salad placed in front you as you lounge around the dinner table following a delicious meal. The aroma fills your nostrils with the odour of a blend of fresh fruit. As you peer into the bowl, the distinct items that make up this salad are obvious, yet its odour is unlike any one fruit. It is a blend of the items in the bowl that creates a beautiful smell. As you dip your spoon into the bowl and raise it toward your mouth you are once again surprised by its exuberant flavour. Each spoonful tickles your pallet in a different way. Each spoonful is different, depending on the blend of fruits that have accumulated upon it. Not one spoonful reflects the taste of just one fruit.

Every individual believer is intended to be a fruit salad. Understandably, this is a statement that requires some explanation. Most Christians have favourite spiritual fruit. It is the fruit they enjoy. It is the fruit they find easiest to bear. As a result, when we speak of bearing fruit their mind immediately goes to their favourite and they think they are doing a great job. The assumption is that if we are bearing one kind of fruit then we are filling the biblical directive to be fruit bearing. That assumption is a dangerous one. Biblically, the Christian life is to be a fruit salad. The Scripture speaks of various kinds of fruit, every one of them an essential part of the Christian life. If we lack one type of fruit we cannot be as potent in our impact. We cannot present the fragrance of God to the world around us. The world will not experience the flavour of Christianity that will be as attractive as the complete salad. Each fruit is both the result of a worshipful life and is an act of worship it itself.

Fruit of the Holy Spirit

Perhaps the most logical fruit to begin with is with the Fruit of the Holy Spirit. It is not the purpose of this book to present a detailed discussion on each of these, but a cursory definition may be of value. Here is the list as it is given by the apostle Paul: "But the fruit of the Spirit is love, joy, peace, patience, kindness, goodness, faithfulness, gentleness and self-control. Against such things there is no law." (Galatians 5:22-23, NIV).

Love. This is the kind of love that will cause you to give completely of yourself for those who are completely undeserving. It is a willful act that motivates us into action. In fact, it is a love that requires active demonstration. It is Calvary kind of love. (I John 3:16).

Joy. The joy given by the Holy Spirit holds us steady through the deepest of trials. It is a supernatural relief relative to the circumstances we face. It doesn't mean that we won't feel the sting of the trial, but this joy finds its roots in the assurance that we will have grown in our relationship with Christ, and in His likeness, when we come out at the other end of it. (James 1:2-4).

Peace. This is a peace that is beyond man's natural ability to understand. It is rooted in absolute confidence in God's ability and desire to care for us no matter what the circumstance. This is the peace of God found only by establishing peace with God. Those who do not have faith in Him are totally incapable of relating to such absolute assurance. (Philippians 4:7).

Patience. This word speaks of endurance. Christ has won the war, but we continue to face daily battles. Christ endured to the cross, not allowing the frustration of life to distract him from His ultimate goal. So will the fruit bearing believer. (Hebrews 12:2-3).

Kindness. This is an active expression of the unconditional love of God. It practically and tangibly acts upon love and reveals to others the love that Christ has put in our hearts. (I Thessalonians 2:7-8).

Goodness. The Greek word used here speaks of action toward moral uprightness. It is not always the kindly kind of goodness mentioned previously, but it may result in tough love. It was this kind of goodness that motivated Christ to purge the temple of the buyers and the sellers in Matthew 21:12-13.

Faithfulness. The King James translation, "faith" seems to be a more accurate translation of the original text. In simple terms it means to trust God. It must be said, however, that simple trust in God is perhaps the catalyst to the most effective and faithful ministry. Jesus' faith in His Heavenly Father and trust in the Holy Spirit to work through Him was simple enough to equip Him for a faithful and powerful ministry. It motivated Him to heal countless people, cast out demons by the legion, walk on water, and change the course of nature.

Gentleness. Sometimes translated meekness, neither English word does real justice to its meaning. It is a character trait that relates first and foremost to our relationship with God, accepting that His dealings with us are always for our ultimate good. As a result of this absolute confidence in Him we are void of self-interest and self-assertion in our interaction with our fellow man.

Self-Control. This is to be in control of one's physical and intellectual being. It is the ability to consistently do what is right, and not do what is wrong. Christ was such a perfect example of this throughout His life and ministry. In the desert temptations, recorded in Matthew 4, Christ exercised both physical and intellectual endurance to win a spiritual victory. (Hebrews 4:15).

When we read the Apostle Paul's list of fruit in Galatians 5:22-23, we don't think of it as being quite as spiritual as, say, the list of the gifts of the Holy Spirit given in 1 Corinthians 12: 8-10. These fruits seem almost mundane. They seem like normal things that most of humanity consider to be desirable characteristics. As a race created in the image of God, there is a natural impulse to be drawn to the characteristics that are rooted in our creator. As Christians, however, we must look for these Godly characteristics to be present in our lives in supernatural quality and quantity. Let there be no mistake. Bearing such fruit is not only fundamental to the Christian life, but it is also the most spiritual of the goals for us to try to attain. This is the character of Christ. These are the fruits that should naturally result from having the Spirit of God dwelling in us. We must bear this fruit beyond man's natural ability. This is true because our very soul has been fertilized by the water of the Holy Spirit. Every one of these qualities must be present in our character to a supernatural degree in order to reflect the presence of Christ in us. It is what separates the multitude of good people in this world from those who truly reveal the nature of God. That is what makes this fruit so spiritual; they reflect the personality of Christ. After all, they are the fruit of Christ's Spirit in us.

Let me show you how essential this fruit is in comparison to things often considered more spiritual. Paul reveals the principle in the renowned love chapter, I Corinthians 13. "If I could speak all the languages of earth and of angels, but didn't love others, I would only be a noisy gong or a clanging cymbal. If I had the gift of prophecy, and if I understood all of God's secret plans and possessed all knowledge, and if I had such faith that I could move mountains, but didn't love others, I would be nothing. If I gave everything I have to the poor and even sacrificed my body, I could boast about it; but if I didn't love others, I would have gained nothing." (1 Corinthians 13:1-3, NLT). The apostle teaches us that the gifts of the Spirit are nullified in their value if the fruit is not present first. Even our apparent acts of kindness mean nothing if our heart is not consistent with the heart of God.

I am the self-proclaimed crokinole champion of the world. Crokinole is a fun game invented in Canada that, admittedly, many Canadians have never even played. I have no trophy, no belt, no ribbon, and no certificate. There are certainly much better crokinole players than me, but I choose not to believe it. That's what it means to be "self-proclaimed". I suppose I have lost my title, since Mr. Pointer has not struck the edge of a crokinole for some years. I used to love the game. The way we kept score in crokinole is that one player always ended the game with a score of zero. We would establish an overall score that would determine a winner, perhaps one hundred. If in one game I concluded with forty points and my opponent concluded with twenty, his score would be zero and mine would be twenty. His points would cancel some of mine. If the opponent won the next game by fifteen, his overall score would remain at zero while mine would be reduced to five. His points cancelled mine. The illustration breaks down quickly I know. At least I got to publicly claim my title. Still, I trust my point is clear.

You can do all of the "spiritual" looking things, but if you are not a spiritual person the value of the activity is cancelled out. If you pray for the sick and they are healed, then proclaim: "Look what I did!", then God has received no glory. The eyes of the onlooker have been taken off of the miracle worker and have been directed to the broken, earthen vessel that was simply an instrument honoured to be used of God. What a shame! The value of the miracle has been cancelled out by the degree of your pride. If you gossip throughout the week, then speak prophetically for God on Sunday, the listeners will see no love in your character and will not hear the message. What a shame! The value of the message has been cancelled by the degree of your lovelessness.

Christianity requires both doing and being. The Christian life is incomplete otherwise. After receiving the free gift of salvation, working for Christ is a must. Hear what Paul teaches in Romans 2:5b "For a day of anger is coming, when God's righteous judgment will be revealed. He will judge everyone according to what they have done. He will give eternal life to those who keep on doing good, seeking after the glory and honor and immortality that God offers. But he will pour out his anger and wrath on those who live for themselves, who refuse to obey the truth and instead live lives of wickedness." (Romans 2:5-8, NLT).

Understand this: You can't do without being, and you can't be without doing. If you try doing Christian things before bearing the fruit of Christ's nature they are done for little or no value. If you concentrate on bearing the fruit of the Holy Spirit, however, doing Christ's work will flow out of that character. The character of Christ motivates us to do the work of Christ. The fruit of our doing will be born out of the fruit of our being. As someone wisely pointed out, you can't get an orange from an apple tree. To do the work of Christ we must become like Christ. All else is for selfish gain. "But he will pour out his anger and wrath on those who live for themselves." (Romans 2:8, NLT).

So, developing the fruit of the Holy Spirit is most essential to the effectiveness of our spiritual lives. Let's take a brief look at how some of these characteristics were revealed to a supernatural degree through the life of Christ.

I need only to lead you to the story of Jesus speaking to a Samaritan woman at a well. You will find the story in John chapter 4. Many Jews considered themselves to be defiled if they came in contact with Samaritans. That is why, when traveling from southern Israel to the north, they would often cross the Jordan River to avoid traveling through the region of Samaria. Not only that, the woman in question had lived a grossly immoral life. She was socially less than desirable. Jesus, however, went out of His way to create the opportunity to offer her springs of living water. In this story we see the characteristics of love, patience, gentleness, goodness, and faithfulness flowing out of Christ and bearing eternal fruit.

Mary Magdalene, honoured to be the first to have had a private audience with the risen Christ, had at one time been possessed by seven demons (Mark 16:9). To that point, she wasn't the type that most embraced as a dear friend. The supernatural character of Christ was able to do so.

Matthew, one of the twelve, had been a despised tax collector previous to Christ's invitation. Christ supernaturally loved him and invited him into His inner circle.

To the adulteress woman, required to die by stoning according to Jewish law, Jesus offered forgiveness (John 8:3-11). We not only see love here, but patience, gentleness, and goodness.

Consistently Christ proved His character to be beyond natural. Ultimately, this character caused Him to go to the cross on which He died. He told us that we too must live a life beyond normal. It is a life that only comes by dying to self. "But to you who are willing to listen, I say, love your enemies! Do good to those who hate you. Bless those who curse you. Pray for those who hurt you. If someone slaps you on one cheek, offer the other cheek also. If someone demands your coat, offer your shirt also. Give to anyone who asks; and when things are taken away from you, don't try to get them back. Do to others as you would like them to do to you. "If you love only those who love you, why should you get credit for that? Even sinners love those who love them! And if you do good only to those who do good to you, why should you get credit? Even sinners do that much! And if you lend money only to those who can repay you, why should you get credit? Even sinners will lend to other sinners for a full return. "Love your enemies! Do good to them. Lend to them without expecting to be repaid. Then your reward from heaven will be very great, and you will truly be acting as children of the Most High, for he is kind to those who are unthankful and wicked. You must be compassionate, just as your Father is compassionate." (Luke 6:27-36, NLT)

It is essential to also understand that as necessary as the fruit of the Holy Spirit is to the work of God, another fruit precedes it. The fruit of the Holy Spirit is the fruit of another fruit.

The Fruit of Righteousness

It starts with relationship with Jesus Christ. Upon accepting Christ as our Saviour, we stand as righteous before God. The Heavenly Father looks at us through the holiness and perfection of His Son and views us through His perfection. That is what makes the hope of entry into heaven as our eternal home possible. God sees us as righteous through Christ. However, there is a responsibility placed on us to allow the righteousness of Christ to flow through our lives in very practical ways.

The Apostle Paul spoke of the fruit of righteousness in Philippians 1:9-11 "I pray that your love will overflow more and more, and that you will keep on growing in knowledge and understanding. For I want you to understand what really matters, so that you may live pure and blameless lives until the day of Christ's return. May you always be filled with the fruit of your salvation—the righteous character produced in your life by Jesus Christ—for this will bring much glory and praise to God." (Philippians 1:9-11, NLT) The fruit of our salvation begins with a righteous standing before the Heavenly Father. Paul teaches here, however, that if this relationship is real it will bear another fruit – the fruit of righteous character. That righteous character is the very nature of Jesus Christ at work in us and through us. The word righteousness means to live a life that is consistent with Divine law, which was exemplified perfectly in the character of Jesus.

In another passage we are given a simple recipe in the development of Christian character. "In view of all this, make every effort to respond to God's promises. Supplement your faith with a generous provision of moral excellence, and moral excellence with knowledge, and knowledge with self-control, and self-control with patient endurance, and patient endurance with godliness, and godliness with brotherly affection, and brotherly affection with love for everyone. The more you grow like this, the more productive and useful you will be in your knowledge of our Lord Jesus Christ. But those who fail to develop in this way are shortsighted or blind, forgetting that they have been cleansed from their old sins. So, dear brothers and sisters, work hard to prove that you really are among those God has called and chosen. Do these things, and you will never fall away. Then God will give you a grand entrance into the eternal Kingdom of our Lord and Savior Jesus Christ." (2 Peter 1:5-11, NLT) This is a powerful text that teaches us about the fruit of righteousness. Peter's instruction here lines up perfectly with the Apostle Paul's. He begins with the righteousness of Christ in us which bears the fruit of moral excellence and the nature of Christ. What stands out here is the emphasis that this requires significant effort on the part of the believer. He says to "supplement our faith" or "add to our faith" moral excellence. He teaches that the more we grow and develop in this the more fruit we will bear, or the more productive we will become. But, we are to "work hard" at this, all "to prove that we really are among those God has called and chosen". This is exactly what Paul was speaking of when he wrote to the Philippian church: "Dear friends, you always followed my instructions when I was with you. And now that I am away, it is even more important. Work hard to show the results of your salvation, obeying God with deep reverence and fear." (Philippians 2:12, NLT)

The character of Christ is born in our hearts at salvation. The potential to live a morally excellent life is immediately present. The seed of Christ's nature is planted in our very beings as the Holy Spirit takes residence in us. At that moment it becomes our responsibility to align our desires and our goals with His nature. More than that, we must make every effort to live a life consistent with the life of Christ in order to bear the fruit of righteousness which leads to the growth of the fruit of the Holy Spirit. Bearing godly fruit comes when the spirit and soul of man are aligned with the Spirit of God who dwells in every believer. It is creating and maintaining that alignment that requires the hard work of which Peter and Paul speak. It is a challenge to be taken on with great reverence for the author of our salvation. It is a challenge to be taken on with a desire to prove to those around us that we truly are His children.

If you have ever driven a car that is seriously out of alignment, you know exactly what this means. The natural inclination of the car is to always go right or left. To make it go straight takes continual effort by the driver. In the same sense, sin has caused our human nature to be out of line with the nature of God. Our natural inclination is toward sin. We are born that way. Our soul has been bent to lead us that direction. Without Christ, we may have a certain understanding of right from wrong. Still, the human nature is driven by selfishness rather than godliness. It is impossible for us to understand true righteousness or Divine law. But when Christ comes into our heart there is a new understanding. There is a desire to live straight. There is awareness of that Divine law that challenges our natural inclinations. We can get there. We can live that way. We can bear the fruit of Christ's nature.

His presence makes the path of righteousness very clear. He puts the lines on life's roadway. But it will take constant effort.

The Fruit of souls

The Apostle Paul's ministry was driven by one thing. We tend to interpret the goals of his ministry by his writings, which fill much of the New Testament. They are full of theology and instruction for the church but Paul was more than just a teacher. The goal of Paul's public ministry was different than that of most of his written works. We see it in this verse: "I want you to know, dear brothers and sisters, that I planned many times to visit you, but I was prevented until now. I want to work among you and see spiritual fruit, just as I have seen among other Gentiles." (Romans 1:13, NLT). What is that spiritual fruit? The New International Version says: "that I might have a harvest among you" (Romans 1:13, NIV). This great man was motivated by the simple gospel message so that souls would be won for the kingdom of God. He reminded the Corinthian Christians of this. "When I first came to you, dear brothers and sisters, I didn't use lofty words and impressive wisdom to tell you God's secret plan. For I decided that while I was with you I would forget everything except Jesus Christ, the one who was crucified." (1 Corinthians 2:1-2, NLT). It was this message that caused him to be run out of towns. This preaching put him in prison shackles on various occasions and for extended periods. It resulted in him being beaten and left for dead. He preached it to kings and paupers alike. In the end, Paul died because he lived to tell the simple truth of the gospel.

Jesus did many things. He healed countless people who were sick and diseased. He performed miracles. He cast out demons. He taught great truths. He drew large crowds to hear Him speak. Everything He did, however, led up to one event. Jesus came to earth for one primary purpose – the cross. Everything else either validated His work on the cross, or His work on the cross validated the things that He said or did. His death was central to His life. His death is the kingpin of the Old Testament and the New Testament. But His death wasn't just about dying. It was about resurrection. It was about life. It was about being the ransom for sin that all men might have the hope of life eternal. It was about fruit. "For God loved the world so much that he gave his one and only Son, so that everyone who believes in him will not perish but have eternal life. God sent his Son into the world not to judge the world, but to save the world through him." (John 3:16-17, NLT) Christ's coming to earth, His life, His death, and His resurrection were all about one thing – that everyone who believes in Him would have eternal life.

If this is true of Christ, and we are His followers, it seems only logical that our entire lives be driven by the desire to see souls born into the kingdom of God. It must be our goal that this be the fruit of all other fruit. Whatever ministry we have, the end goal must be the salvation of souls. Whatever ministry activity we are involved in, the end goal must be that others would come into the kingdom of God. Even if our ministry is to believers, our goal must be that they be better equipped to lead people to Christ. Salvation of souls should be the fruit of all other fruit. It is what Christ died for. So, it is what we live for.

The fact that we argue over worship style is strong evidence that we have completely lost sight of what real worship is. I said earlier that "All forms of worship that don't lead to fruitful Christianity are essentially practices that are self-satisfying rather than true acts of worship." Without a doubt, serving Christ is the most satisfying thing any man or woman could ever do. Any real Christian will tell you that being in relationship with God brings a hope, purpose, and fulfilment that cannot be found elsewhere. That satisfaction, however, comes from relationship with God, not from enjoying personal preference in how the church goes about its business. Out of that relationship, flows fruit bearing worship, which is not a style of singing. It is a style of living. It is not an order of service; it is an order of life. For this to happen we will bear the fruit of our salvation, which is righteousness. In turn the fruit of righteousness is the character of Christ. And when His character is presented to the world without blemish many will long to know Him personally. That's the kind of 'fruit salad' the church needs. Any other kind of Christianity is just nuts.

2 YOU ARE WHAT YOU EAT

I have anything but a green thumb, but I do know that sick plants don't bear good fruit if they bear fruit at all. The fruit of an ill or malnourished plant is often small and unattractive. If the plant is really sick, or poorly fed, the plant will funnel every ounce of nourishment toward simply staying alive and will bear no fruit.

There is a riveting story found in II Kings 6:24 – 7:20. It is a story full of desperate people. Not only were they not bearing good fruit, it was a fight for survival. They were starving and doing their best to stay alive. It wasn't going very well.

I would like to analyze this story so that we can see how consuming the wrong food affects our ability to bear fruit. Of course, I'm not talking about literal food. I'm talking about those things we feed our soul; the things we take in through our senses that contribute to who we become spiritually and emotionally. Ultimately these things shape our personality. It is necessary for us to understand that the person we are spiritually and emotionally determines the nature and the quality of the fruit that we bear. What we take in through our senses feeds and shapes our nature as a fruit bearer. Since the spirit and emotions are often in control of our personality, this is of huge importance. When we feed our spirit godly things it is easier to bear godly fruit. It is easier to bear the fruit of our salvation, which is righteousness. Out of that flows the character of

Jesus as seen in our supernatural levels of joy, peace, longsuffering, gentleness, goodness, faith, meekness, and temperance. The spirit controls the human nature. This can be true in the negative sense as well. If we feed on ungodly things, it makes sense that we will not bear the fruit of our salvation but of the sinful nature. Sin will increase in our lives. If we feed on things that are neither right or wrong, godly or ungodly, we simply starve ourselves spiritually. These things provide no nourishment. As a result, our ability to bear fruit will diminish and eventually we will move into a state where we are merely fighting to survive spiritually, bearing no good fruit at all.

The characters in our story are desperate people. It is very interesting to analyze their responses to their desperate situation.

The threat of Aramean attack had been hanging over the heads of the people of Samaria for some time. Tension had been building. Finally, under the leadership of King Ben Hadad, the Aramean army pushed their way to the gates of Samaria. Ben Hadad controlled all roads to the city. All supply routes were cut off. It seemed rather obvious that the defeat of the Samaritans was just a matter of time. The Arameans had laid siege to the city. They would simply wait for the king of Samaria to announce his surrender.

The end was very close. Food inside the city of Samaria was nearly impossible to get. What they could get was extremely costly. The head of a donkey could be purchased for the ridiculous price of eight shekels of silver. My mind wants to wonder about what kind of dinner you would make with the head of a donkey. Unfortunately, my imagination causes my soup to look back at me, so we'd better not allow my imagination to go too far. You could buy one quarter of a cab of seedpods for five shekels of silver. I understand that in more common vernacular, this is about one-half pint of dove's dung. I'm trying not to imagine this on toast. As much as I jest, this indicates the seriousness of their situation. It was dire.

Even this does not quite reflect the horrors that went on in the city. Some had even resorted to cannibalism. Two women had made an unbelievably inhumane arrangement. The first lady said to the second: "Come on, let's eat your son today, then we will eat my son tomorrow." (2 Kings 6:28, NLT). It is an unthinkable proposal. Still, out of desperation, in a selfish act to preserve her own life, the second lady agreed. She killed her son and they ate him that day. In the meantime, the lady who made the proposal had no intention of killing her child. She hid her boy, and there was no food for the next day.

The lady who killed and ate her child was beside herself. She reported this event to the Samarian king, King Jehoram. Jehoram was the son and product of a very evil royal couple, Ahab and Jezebel. But even such an evil king was horrified by what he heard. His spirit was broken. He tore his kingly robes, revealing that he was wearing sackcloth underneath. Sackcloth was a sign of being in mourning. Now it was public that King Jehoram was in mourning for his city.

Sadness often looks for a place to blame. Jehoram's mother, Jezebel, was famous for blaming the great prophet Elijah when things went wrong. Consistent with his upbringing, Jehoram decides that this must be the man of God, Elisha's fault. There seemed to have been a belief that these prophets didn't just speak for God, but that they empowered their own prophetic messages. In any case, King Jehoram wanted Elisha's head, and he wanted it today!

Elisha is alerted by the Holy Spirit of this plot against his life. King Jehoram sent a messenger to Elisha's home. His task was to return with Elisha's head. Elisha was there with the elders of the city. I have no idea what they were doing, but I imagine them sitting around the kitchen table drinking coke and playing checkers. There is a possibility that I am wrong about that. Whatever they were doing, Elisha has the men that are with him hold the door shut so that the king's hit man cannot enter. At some point the king decides to follow. When he arrives at Elisha's home, he poses a simple question for Elisha. "All this misery is from the LORD! Why should I wait for the LORD any longer?" (2 Kings 6:33, NLT). It is an interesting question that both blames God and views Him as the solution to their desperate situation.

Have you ever felt that way? Have you ever been in a situation where you have absolutely no solution of your own? And, in that situation you wonder how long you have to wait for God to come to your rescue? Jehoram was in that place.

The question is: What do you feed yourself during desperate times in your life? How do you sustain yourself spiritually? What are your comfort foods? Desperate circumstances can actually be a positive point in time if our desperation drives us closer to our creator and the one who sustains us in every circumstance. It can be a positive thing if we are reminded that God is our only source of sustenance, the only real and lasting solution to our problem, the only one who can provide for our need. If our desperation makes us hungry for spiritually solid food, and for the person of God, it has been a positive point in our lives.

We can't forget that in some people's lives, the best of times is the worst of times for them spiritually. It is when everything is going well that they forget their need for God and become spiritually destitute. It is a different form of desperate situation, but it is desperation none-the-less. The same questions regarding what you feed yourself spiritually need to be asked, even when all of the outward circumstances are just fine.

If the church is going to bear kingdom fruit in a significant way, we need to get to the place where we hunger and thirst after everything righteous whether in good times or bad. We must get to where we long for those things that will nourish our spirits and feed our souls. We must get to the place where we are desperate for God and all things godly.

The Present State of the Church

There are signs that would suggest that the flow of God's fruit bearing Spirit in the church has diminished. I believe it has been the enemy's tactic to so fill us up with spiritual junk food that we have no room for the good food God has for us.

I want you to be certain of one thing as we launch into this subject. God's resources have not diminished. The supply of God's Holy Spirit remains unlimited. The Holy Spirit is not getting old and powerless. The winds of the Holy Spirit are blowing as strongly as ever. The fire of the Holy Spirit burns as brightly as it ever has. The river of God's Spirit flows freely. It is evident, however, that the enemy has placed a stranglehold on the church in some ways. There are things that have cut off the flow of the Holy Spirit into the church. I know this, because when I read of the church in Acts chapters 2 to 10 and compare it to the church today, there are few similarities in terms of the volume and nature of the fruit we bear.

The world, over which Satan is its prince (John 12:31), has pushed its' way to the very gates of the church. In some cases it has infiltrated today's religion. People living extra-biblical and ungodly lifestyles preach from Christian pulpits. Relationships that include sexual intimacy outside of marriage are viewed as acceptable by some. Physical, emotional, and sexual abuse is a real problem even in so-called Christian homes. These are obvious signs, but there are others that I would like to address in more detail.

Starving Christians

There are many Christians that are starving to death. It isn't because they haven't been filling themselves up, but they have been feeding on things that have no spiritual nutritional value. They have been busy, they have been entertained, and they go to bed at night feeling that they have lived a full life.

Let me tell you that the enemy has used our quest for material things, television, internet activities, sports, etc. to replace good spiritual food. These are the donkey's heads and the dove's dung of the 21st Century. They aren't necessarily bad, but they are no substitute for real spiritual food.

Sustenance comes to our spirit through the study of God's Word and through spending time in His presence. But it seems that many feel this good food is too costly. They can't afford the time. The junk food of today doesn't satisfy for long, but it is cheap and tasty. Material things make us appear successful and satisfy a certain temporal desire. Sitting in front of the television or the computer is much easier than reading God's Word. Going to a ball game takes much less effort than spending time in prayer.

Please don't misunderstand me. I am not against making ourselves comfortable by having a nice home and nice things. I am not anti-television. I particularly enjoy watching something that will make me laugh, something that will distract me from the pressures of the day. I have nothing against computers or the internet. I believe that the internet is an invaluable source of information and even communication. Neither am I anti-sports. I love sports! If people are competing at something, I enjoy watching them. I enjoy the competition and I respect those who try so hard to be the best at what they do.

However, if we work continuous overtime and double shifts just to attain 'things' and don't feed on spiritual food, we have mixed up priorities. If we can find three hours to watch a football or baseball game, and cannot find half hour to read God's Word, we have a serious problem. If we can sit in front of the computer or television and go brain dead for hours on end, and not spend significant quality time in God's presence we are not going to bear godly fruit. We will, however, starve ourselves to death spiritually. It doesn't matter what the activity is, if we prefer feeding ourselves on that rather than the good food God has given us, we will bear little fruit and are in serious spiritual danger.

Eating our Babies

I don't mean to shock you, but many Christians are cannibalistic. They are devouring one another. In-house bickering and dissent is rampant in the church today. How, on earth, does the church ever expect to bear good spiritual fruit when we can't even get along amongst ourselves?

If I were to ask you how you would feel about having an orgy as a church activity, you would probably throw me out the door and have a restraining order placed against me. If I suggested we have a drunken party at the church, the response would likely be the same. Apparently in the minds of many, however, causing dissention in the church is perfectly acceptable. The apostle Paul, under the inspiration of the Holy Spirit, seems to feel that there is no difference. "Let us behave decently, as in the daytime, not in orgies and drunkenness, not in sexual immorality and debauchery, not in dissension and jealousy. Rather, clothe yourselves with the Lord Jesus Christ, and do not think about how to gratify the desires of the sinful nature." (Romans 13:13-14, NIV). Isn't it interesting that these things get lumped together in this verse? They are all described as gratification of the sinful nature. Doesn't this passage suggest that Paul views all of the activities listed as equally disgusting? In Proverbs 16:28, Solomon says: "A perverse man stirs up dissension, and a gossip separates close friends." (Proverbs 16:28, NIV). Earlier in the book, Solomon says that there are six things that God hates and seven that are detestable. The seventh thing mentioned is dissention (Proverbs 6:16-19).

Division and dissention in the church make God sick! It is a sign of man's emptiness and sadness that seeks someone else to blame, just like King Jehoram sought after Elisha to blame him for his problems. It is a sign of man trying to express his own emptiness by hurting someone else rather than turning to God to find spiritual nourishment and strength. Sometimes people are so spiritually empty, and they hurt so badly, that they try to make themselves feel better by making someone else feel worse.

Often church is a place where people either seek or have opportunity for leadership positions. That occasionally turns into an opportunity to control rather than lead. If leaders have wrong motives, or don't have a servant's heart, division often starts right there. I think there must be times when King Jesus takes off His Kingly robes and reveals that He is in mourning for the church divided.

The apostle, John, joins Solomon and Paul in addressing this most serious subject. In I John 4:20 he writes: " If someone says, "I love God," but hates a Christian brother or sister, that person is a liar; for if we don't love people we can see, how can we love God, whom we cannot see?" (1 John 4:20, NLT). (Please also read I John 2:9-11 and I John 3:14-16).

The church, all too often, makes spiritual babies by telling people that God loves them. People are born into the family of God and come into the church because it is supposed to be a place where this love of God is reflected. Then we destroy them by our lack of love and our critical spirits. The fruit cannot survive the hostile environment of the church. We eat our babies.

If we view the church as a body, as Scripture does, we can see how ridiculous dissention in the body really is. It is no different than the person who bangs their head against a wall or slashes him or herself. There is something sick inside that individual that makes them want to punish or hurt another part of their body. A sore head doesn't help a sick mind, but somehow hurting another part of the body appeases the part of that individual that is sick. If you desire to hurt someone else in the body of Christ, you are the sick part of the body! You need spiritual medicine to make you better. You need to be in the Word of God seeking what it has to say about how we should treat one another. Hurting another part of the body will not help you. Hurting someone else only serves to hurt someone else. When you do so, you are literally hurting the head of the church. You are hurting Jesus Christ.

If you look at others in the church with a desire to hurt and devour, it is time to check what you have been feeding yourself. You are a starving believer. The fruit of your desires and behaviour are not consistent with godly food. I guarantee you that you have not been feeding on God's Word because His Word does not allow spiritual cannibalism. You have not been in His presence enough to be filled up with His love and forgiving attitude. You are not bearing the fruit of the Holy Spirit.

Unbelievable Blessing

The promises of God are so incredible that they are almost hard to believe at times. John the Baptist prophesied that: "someone is coming soon who is greater than I am—so much greater that I'm not worthy even to be his slave and carry his sandals. He will baptize you with the Holy Spirit and with fire." (Matthew 3:11, NLT).

Even more incredibly, Jesus said: "I tell you the truth, anyone who believes in me will do the same works I have done, and even greater works, because I am going to be with the Father. You can ask for anything in my name, and I will do it, so that the Son can bring glory to the Father. Yes, ask me for anything in my name, and I will do it!" (John 14:12-14, NLT) These are incredible promises that ensure us that spiritual life will flow through our veins to bear remarkable fruit. He will immerse us in the Holy Spirit and set us ablaze for Him. We, the church, should be able to do what Jesus did and bear the same fruit. Did you see that in the Scripture? Do you even attempt to comprehend it, or does your mind immediately dismiss its application to you personally? I'm guessing that some reading this book are already making excuses as to why these things are not a reality in the church today and why they are not bearing the fruit of Christ's power that is available to us.

As our mind returns to the biblical story, the prophet Elisha prophesies something unbelievable. He says that in twenty-four hours, food will be plentiful and will be available at a reasonable price. In the natural, this would be a literal impossibility. It just couldn't happen. In fact, the messenger that was sent to kill Elisha scoffed at the prophecy. He said: "That couldn't happen even if the LORD opened the windows of heaven!" (2 Kings 7:2, NLT). Elisha, not impressed by this lack of faith, responded: "You will see it happen with your own eyes, but you won't be able to eat any of it!" (2 Kings 7:2, NLT). Here is what happened: King Jehoram had reached a place where he didn't know how to react. In his mind he had two choices. He could continue to blame this entire situation on Elisha and kill him right then and there. Or, he could listen to this prophecy and wait twenty-four hours to see what happens. Wisely, he chose the latter.

Outside the city walls were four men with leprosy. You wouldn't think so, but these men were in a very positive position. If they stayed where they were they would die as unfed beggars. No one had a morsel to give them. Going inside the city was against the law for people in their physical condition. In the city they would either die with the rest of the people or be killed. Their only other option was to go down to the camp of the enemy; the Arameans. Their advantage was their desperation. They had nothing to lose. Their desperation caused them to do something they wouldn't normally do. It is commonly said that "desperate men take desperate measures".

Desperation is often brought on by circumstances. When it comes to our desire for God, it neither has to be that way nor should it be that way. Desperation for God should be an attitude of the heart. I can imagine the psalmist, just before penning Psalm 42. I imagine him sitting very still near a desert stream, contemplating life or pondering the things of God. As he sits quietly, he hears a rustle in one of the sparse shrubs nearby. As he turns, with a bit of a start, he sees a small deer that had been wandering through the desert. It was so needy of something to drink. As it approached the edge of the stream, the song writer could see its chest expanding and contracting in desperation for the water just ahead. Finally, reaching the water's edge, the sleek creature begins to lap up the fresh, cool water. Its panting slows as its body is satisfied by the stream's provision. Immediately the psalmist begins to write: "As the deer longs for streams of water, so I long for you, O God. I thirst for God, the living God. When can I go and stand before him?" (Psalm 42:1-2, NLT). What I imagine the psalmist witnessing is a mental picture of how he felt about God. The writer, obviously a man with a deep passion for the things of God, longed to be in His presence. His soul literally panted for the presence of His Lord and His friend.

The Apostle Paul expressed his longing in different words, although the desire was the same. "I want to know Christ and experience the mighty power that raised him from the dead. I want to suffer with him, sharing in his death, so that one way or another I will experience the resurrection from the dead! I don't mean to say that I have already achieved these things or that I have already reached perfection. But I press on to possess that perfection for which Christ Jesus first possessed me." (Philippians 3:10-12, NLT). This is Paul speaking. He had unbelievable encounters with the risen Christ. He had seen untold miracles and was considered a leader among Christian leaders. Still, he writes: "I want to know Christ". "I press on". Once again we see one of the great heroes of the faith expressing an unquenchable hunger after God.

This kind of desperation leads us to the place of spiritual sustenance, nourishment, and strength. We must become desperate for God and desperate to be kingdom fruit-bearers to the point where we will do something we wouldn't normally do – just like the lepers did. We need to do whatever it takes to get into God's presence and His Word. We are what we eat. As we satisfy ourselves in this way we are guaranteed to bear the fruit of righteousness, the fruit of the Spirit, and bring a harvest of souls.

The end of the biblical story is quite remarkable. The four lepers nervously approach the Aramean camp. As they get closer they come to the realization that there is no one around. God had caused them to hear the sound of chariots, horses and a great army. They reasoned that King Jehoram had established a treaty with the Hittites and the Egyptians, and that this alliance was attacking them. So the Arameans ran for their lives. They left all of their belongings behind. They left their tents, their drink, their silver, their gold, their clothing, and most importantly; their food. The lepers were not concerned about whether or not there was food and supplies there. They were concerned about whether or not the Arameans would accept them. God supernaturally took care of that.

In the same way, God has made a supernatural way to the provision He has for us. At the cross of Calvary, He made the way of salvation. He was resurrected and later ascended into heaven so that He could send His Holy Spirit to fill and empower us. All that we need to become all that God wants us to be, so that we can do all that God want us to do, is available in His presence. Provision is not a problem. Not only that, God has supernaturally made the way possible for us to 'come and get it'. Still, so many choose to feed on today's junk food and wonder why they are not bearing spiritual fruit. They are not taking advantage of what is readily available in God presence.

Blessing is for Blessing

The four lepers couldn't believe it. They went into one of the tents and began enjoying all that was there for them. They even hid some things for later. Then they went to another tent and did the same. Soon they realized something vitally important. They were wrong to keep this to themselves. The provision was there for everyone. When are we as a church going to allow this truth to get past our brain and into our hearts? What God has made available is not just for us. It is for everyone. It is so wrong to find our way into a relationship with God, to find the hope of eternal life; and keep it to ourselves. We must stop hiding this truth. Jesus knew this would be a problem, so He addressed it. He said: "No one lights a lamp and then hides it or puts it under a basket. Instead, a lamp is placed on a stand, where its light can be seen by all who enter the house." (Luke 11:33, NLT). To not lead others to the provision made available through Christ is the most selfish act one could possibly commit.

The lepers went to the gate keepers and told them what they had discovered. News was sent to the palace. The king was cautious, and wisely sent out two chariots with their riders to find the Aramean army. The story they were told by the lepers was true. They found the road littered with clothing and equipment all the way down to the Jordan River. God had miraculously provided! All of the people went out of the city and plundered the Aramean army without so much as a sword having to be drawn. The messenger who had doubted Elisha's prophecy of this event was standing at the city gates and was trampled as people scrambled for the good food. He died. Elisha's prophecy was accurate once again. If you're not going to go to the place of God's miraculous provision, if you are not going to partake of the good fruit so that you can become a good fruit bearer, at least don't stand in the way of those who are. It's a very dangerous place to be.

God has not only made salvation available to us, but everything else that we need to become powerful fruit bearing Christians. But it is just not happening. In many cases it is because Christians are feeding on twenty-first century junk food and ignoring all that God has made available to us through His Word and His Spirit. Do you cringe when you read these words from the book of Hebrews? " You have been believers so long now that you ought to be teaching others. Instead, you need someone to teach you again the basic things about God's word. You are like babies who need milk and cannot eat solid food. For someone who lives on milk is still an infant and doesn't know how to do what is right. Solid food is for those who are mature, who through training have the skill to recognize the difference between right and wrong." (Hebrews 5:12-14, NLT). The writer is speaking of the truths of God's Word. It is truth for the mind and food for the soul. Every believer needs a steady and daily diet of His Word in order to be spiritually nourished, and to reach maturity as a believer. Spending time in God's presence is sustenance for the Spirit. Every believer needs to feast on His presence regularly in order to be strong in Spirit. The hours we spend in front of certain television shows, on certain web sites, secular books, and sporting activities fill our mind and spirit with junk food at the very least. Often, what is found in those places can be toxic to our spirit. The quest for earthly things consumes our time and establishes idols in our lives that take our focus off of our biblical responsibilities. If the fruit of our life is going to be consistent with the character of Christ, we must go on a spiritual diet. We must eat what is good for the soul.

Everything we need to be an effective, fruit bearing believer is freely available to us. Heed the invitation of the prophet Isaiah: "Is anyone thirsty? Come and drink—even if you have no money. Come, take your choice of wine or milk—it's all free! Why spend your money on food that does not give you strength? Why pay for food that does you no good? Listen to me, and you will eat what is good. You will enjoy the finest food." (Isaiah 55:1-2, NLT)

3 HERE COMES JESUS

To say that Jesus is the perfect example in bearing fruit would be ludicrous. After all, Jesus was the perfect example in everything. Still, there are some things about the Son of God that we must analyze to help us understand our place and responsibility as fruit-bearers.

Our historical record of Jesus portrays Him as a sandal wearing, long haired, robe clad gentle man who wandered the hills of Galilee teaching people and performing miracles. There is nothing wrong with this vision. It is all true. But our awareness of who Jesus is cannot begin and end there. Even though we know better intellectually, this vision of Christ limits our thinking regarding the sacrifice He made. We tend to focus on Him sacrificing His humanity for our salvation. Again, this is absolutely true. He did. But the sacrifice of Christ began long before that. Before sacrificing His humanity, He had to set aside His Divinity. What an incredible price He paid for our salvation.

Jesus Before Us

The Scripture is clear. Jesus is, and always was, God. The doctrine of the Trinity challenges our limited ability to understand, simply because our mind attempts to complicate it. The Scriptural truth is that three distinct entities operate in perfect unity as one God: Father, Son, and Holy Spirit. It is as simple as that. Jesus is God.

The apostle John penned some incredible words not recorded by the other Gospel writers. He was one of the twelve disciples who spent the entire three years of Jesus' ministry travelling with Him and devouring His truths. He was very close to Jesus (John 19:26, 21:20). This intimacy afforded him opportunities to see and hear things that some of the others didn't. He spoke out of experiences that some of the others didn't have. He was one of three that saw the glory of God shining through Jesus on the mountain top. Jesus' face became like the sun, and His clothes like the light. He had a glimpse of Jesus' true nature. Out of his experiences and knowledge, John wrote: "In the beginning the Word already existed. The Word was with God, and the Word was God. He existed in the beginning with God. God created everything through him, and nothing was created except through him. The Word gave life to everything that was created, and his life brought light to everyone. The light shines in the darkness, and the darkness can never extinguish it." (John 1:1-5, NLT)

Before time existed, Jesus did. He was with God in the beginning. He was God in the beginning. He was and is part of the triune God. When the words rung out through absolute darkness; "Let there be light", they were Jesus' words. When God said: "Let us make human beings in our image, to be like us." (Genesis 1:26, NLT). Jesus' voice blended with the voices of the Father and the Spirit to speak humanity into existence.

The apostle Paul said it this way: "Christ is the visible image of the invisible God. He existed before anything was created and is supreme over all creation, for through him God created everything in the heavenly realms and on earth. He made the things we can see and the things we can't see - such as thrones, kingdoms, rulers, and authorities in the unseen world. Everything was created through him and for him. He existed before anything else, and he holds all creation together." (Colossians 1:15-17, NLT). It is important to understand this truth about Jesus for a multitude of reasons. One of those reasons has to do with you being a fruit-bearer. We'll discuss this in a moment.

Jesus With Us

The truth is that the rightful home of the same Jesus that we envision wandering the hillsides and dusty roadways of ancient Israel is a place that is glorious beyond our imagination. In that place, He has supreme authority. His seat is a throne. Myriads of angels worship Him. He is so mighty and so powerful that creation is in His very words. The laws of this world, such as gravity and physics, were created by Him. They do not restrict Him. He doesn't strive for equality with God because He is God. But He was willing to set that all aside. He left heaven for a time and came to live among men so that He might bear the fruit of our salvation. "Though he was God, he did not think of equality with God as something to cling to. Instead, he gave up his divine privileges; he took the humble position of a slave and was born as a human being. When he appeared in human form, he humbled himself in obedience to God and died a criminal's death on a cross." (Philippians 2:6-8, NLT). Hang on to this truth. Move it into the forefront of your mind. For salvation to be made available to mankind Jesus had to live among men. He had to show us His nature; He had to die.

The hallmark of Jesus' ministry when He was on earth was compassion. When people were sick, diseased, handicapped or injured; He had compassion on them. He broke through the barriers that normal man lives under in this fallen world and He healed them. When people were hungry, He had compassion on them. He miraculously fed them. When people were grieving, He was moved with compassion. In the case of Lazarus, He wept, and then He raised him from the dead. Compassion followed by action - that was Christ's methodology in winning the hearts of men and women. That is what took Him to Calvary. That is why we worship Him today. Compassion followed by action was the methodology of Jesus in bearing spiritual fruit.

Jesus Through Us

Jesus came to earth as a man, not only to die, but to show us His character and to reveal His unconditional love for mankind. If Jesus hadn't lived the life He lived, not so many would pay attention to the death He died. God incarnate is what made salvation possible for any and all of mankind who choose to believe in Him and choose to serve Him. That hasn't changed. Only faith in Jesus' work at Calvary can save men and women. But the responsibility of revealing God's character has shifted. The responsibility of compassion followed by action is now ours. The task of bearing fruit by pointing people to the person and work of Jesus belongs to us.

We are not God. How can we even think of doing what Jesus did? We are mere human beings with a sinful and frail nature. How could we possibly do the work of God incarnate? Before His crucifixion, Jesus gave us the answer: "When I am raised to life again, you will know that I am in my Father, and you are in me, and I am in you." (John 14:20, NLT). The incarnation of Jesus, or the nature of God being seen in the flesh, is now our responsibility. Despite what new age proponents would teach us, we cannot become God. We are not gods. But we have the Spirit of God in us that will enable and empower us to represent the God we serve; to be His likeness on earth. The fruit of the Spirit is not a result of the efforts of the soul; it is the work of God through us.

Just as Jesus set aside privileges and rights as God when He came to earth, we must be willing to set aside those things that hold us back from being good ambassadors of Christ. The things that hold us back are not normally as heavenly the things Jesus set aside. As Christ set aside things that were inherent in His Divine nature, we must be willing to set aside things that are inherent in our human nature. Christ set aside the rights of Divinity so that He could be fully human and experience true humanity. We must set aside aspects of our humanity so that we can accurately represent the person and nature of the Son of God. These things prevent us from representing Jesus through our humanity. If the Son of God can set aside the privileges and rights of being God for this purpose, surely we can set aside the right we have to live according to our human nature. Perhaps the following are some of the common characteristics that we often cling to.

Pride and Insecurity

Pride and insecurity often look so much alike that it is hard to tell the difference. Many people who struggle with insecurity appear to be proud as they constantly build themselves up in the eyes of others. Either way, whether it be pride or insecurity, the reason that they are not open about their relationship with God with others is concern about what those 'others' will think of them. Jesus anticipated this. He attempted to prepare His followers when he gave His 'Sermon at the Mount'. "God blesses you when people mock you and persecute you and lie about you and say all sorts of evil things against you because you are my followers. Be happy about it! Be very glad! For a great reward awaits you in heaven. And remember, the ancient prophets were persecuted in the same way." (Matthew 5:11-12, NLT).

Nobody likes rejection. No one enjoys being laughed at or made fun of. Those things are like a gunshot to one's self esteem. We bleed pride when it happens. Jesus understood that. What He was teaching those on the hillside that day, and us by extension, is to keep your eyes on the prize. He is not encouraging people to seek persecution because they will get a greater reward in heaven. What He is saying is that, when it happens, stay focused on the fact that your attempt at bearing eternal fruit is the will of God; that is worthy of eternal reward. Remember that. Stay focused on that. It is this focus that will stop the bleeding.

Our priorities are a key in this as well. We have to put the importance of others' eternal destiny on one side of the scale and our pride on the other. Is there a contest? Is there any situation where others' opinion about you is more important than their eternal destiny? Absolutely not! So neither pride or insecurity are reason enough not to share the love of Jesus with others, with the hope of bearing eternal fruit.

The Bible has plenty to say about pride. Here is a small sample: "Pride ends in humiliation, while humility brings honour." (Proverbs 29:23, NLT). Another biblical proverb says: "Pride leads to disgrace, but with humility comes wisdom." (Proverbs 11:2, NLT). The message is both simple and clear. Allowing pride to be a controlling factor in our life will not have a good end. It prevents us from representing Christ to the world in an accurate manner. That is Christ, who "took the humble position of a slave" (Philippians 2:7, NLT). It inhibits our ability to bear fruit and robs Christ of the credit for what He has done in our lives. Are you willing to give up your pride for the sake of bearing fruit for the kingdom of God?

Scripture is not silent about insecurity either. It is essential that we be confident because of our relationship with Christ, and because of who we are in Christ. "We are confident of all this because of our great trust in God through Christ. It is not that we think we are qualified to do anything on our own. Our qualification comes from God." (2 Corinthians 3:4-5, NLT). If we are in relationship with Christ and bearing kingdom fruit without the hindrance of insecurity, it is clear that we have confidence in Him. On the other hand, if we are in Christ and not making a strong effort to bear godly fruit because of insecurity, our lack of confidence is really lack of confidence in Him. We don't often think of the fact that how we live our lives is a reflection on our level of faith in God. There is a huge gap in the definitions of meekness and weakness. If Christ is our strength, there is no place for weakness in our life. Paul wrote: "despite all these things, overwhelming victory is ours through Christ, who loved us." (Romans 8:37, NLT). Are you willing to give up your insecurity for the sake of bearing fruit for the Kingdom of God?

Shame

Occasionally one of our most powerful witnessing tools is our largest inhibition. It is our testimony (we will discuss how to use our testimony in Chapter 11). It is very often difficult to share our faith with those that we are close to because they know all of our imperfections. If our past has been rather sordid, this problem may be more acute. Rather than seeing the opportunity to explain the bigness of God's grace, we are inhibited because we are ashamed of how we lived our life prior to our relationship with God. The shame of that old lifestyle causes us to believe that others will see us as hypocritical, or that religion has become a new 'fad' in our life. We fear that some might even think of our relationship with Christ as a crutch or even something that gives us the psychological fortitude to overcome our previous way of living. So we let every opportunity to represent Christ slip through our fingers. No! No matter what we have done, long ago or as recently as today, if we are truly repentant and have given it to God we must not walk through life with shame on our face, but with grace on our lips.

There is a small risk in this teaching. The risk is that even Christians may feel that the greatest way to reveal God's grace is to continue in sin. If that is how you think you have reason to be ashamed. Once we know Christ, we have an obligation to represent His righteousness to the world. The Apostle Paul wrote: "Well then, should we keep on sinning so that God can show us more and more of his wonderful grace? Of course not! Since we have died to sin, how can we continue to live in it?" (Romans 6:1-2, NLT).

Before he was renamed Paul, the apostle's name was Saul. He hated Christians. He was instrumental in Christians being arrested and imprisoned, and was proud of it. He called himself "the worst of sinners". Listen carefully to what this former Christian hater said now that He was a Christian himself: "For I am not ashamed of this Good News about Christ. It is the power of God at work, saving everyone who believes—the Jew first and also the Gentile. This Good News tells us how God makes us right in his sight. This is accomplished from start to finish by faith. As the Scriptures say, "It is through faith that a righteous person has life." (Romans 1:16-17, NLT)

Whatever we have done in our lives that we have confessed before God, and that we have truly repented of, has been wiped from God's memory. "You were dead because of your sins and because your sinful nature was not yet cut away. Then God made you alive with Christ, for he forgave all our sins. He canceled the record of the charges against us and took it away by nailing it to the cross. In this way, he disarmed the spiritual rulers and authorities. He shamed them publicly by his victory over them on the cross." (Colossians 2:13-15, NLT). Rather than us living in shame, Satan should hide his head in humiliation. He was completely humiliated by the work Christ did at the cross. Satan cowers every time you represent Christ and speak of His saving grace. Every time someone is led to Christ Satan is completely put to shame. This effect, however, is nullified if we do not boldly and proudly share Christ so that others might find a victorious life in Jesus. Are you willing to give up your shame for the sake of bearing fruit for the kingdom of God?

Accountability

Openly declaring ourself to be Christian with our words places upon us a responsibility to be Christian in our lifestyle. Sometimes the people around us place a higher standard on the Christian lifestyle than even the church does. One hindrance in being a determined fruit bearer is often because we don't want to give up the freedom to live the way we want, when we want. The openness required to be a successful fruit bearer makes us very accountable to the people around us. They watch us for consistency. They watch to see if our walk lines up with our talk. It is easy to live the Christian life on Sunday when we are sitting in church or hanging out with our church friends. It is not quite so easy on Monday when we are at the rink with the boys, or out with the girls. It is a shame to say that living a double standard is not all that uncommon among believers. It is exactly why many point at the Christian church and cry: "hypocrites". We certainly don't want to be called one of those, so we hide our Christianity under a bushel outside the church.

Jesus often spoke very bluntly. He didn't want the message to be misunderstood. Here is what He had to say on the subject: "Everyone who acknowledges me publicly here on earth, I will also acknowledge before my Father in heaven. But everyone who denies me here on earth, I will also deny before my Father in heaven." (Matthew 10:32-33, NLT). In other words, if we aren't willing to be accountable for our Christianity to the people around us, we will be accountable to Him. The result is not a positive one.

Pastors and church leaders: if we have not presented the importance of being fruit bearing Christians clearly and seriously to our congregations, we have done our people and our world a huge disfavour. Many have cushioned the message to the point where people have become 'okay' with the idea of living their lives for Jesus privately. The message of Christ Himself is that there is no such thing as private Christianity. There is no such thing as a double standard. There is no such thing as being a Sunday Christian. The message of the Scripture is that living for Jesus is a 24/7 proposition. It is to be lived in such a way that our Christianity is visible to everyone, and we represent Christ well in all that we do. Are you willing to give up your desire to be unaccountable to those around you for the sake of bearing fruit for the kingdom of God?

Previous paragraphs almost hints that the salvation of souls is the only fruit of any 'real' value. When we look at Jesus' life, we realize that the salvation of souls was the desired end of His work, but there were vital aspects of what Jesus did that preceded the cross of Calvary. They were things that revealed the nature of God and increased the effectiveness of both His life, and the work accomplished through His death. It was the fruit of His character that bore the fruit of souls.

When Jesus came to earth, His ministry was marked by a few things. Power was one. Authority was another. Compassion was at the core of everything He did. The salvation of mankind was the ultimate goal. Since Jesus now lives in us by His Holy Spirit (John 14:17) it is our responsibility to do the work of Jesus. He prophesied: "I tell you the truth, anyone who believes in me will do the same works I have done, and even greater works, because I am going to be with the Father. You can ask for anything in my name, and I will do it, so that the Son can bring glory to the Father. Yes, ask me for anything in my name, and I will do it!" (John 14:12-14, NLT).

There is one thing that is certain. That is the consistency of the nature of God. Power and authority exercised with compassion, all for the ultimate goal of saving the lost, is what Jesus was all about. It is how He went about His work when He was physically on earth, and it is how He goes about doing His work now that He is here physically through us, the church. The question for us today then is: "How does this play out in our everyday lives and ministries in the 21st century?"

The Scripture above is clear that the power of God is available to us who believe. It is not available to us for selfish benefit. It is available to us to do the will and the work of Jesus. Scripture is also clear that He makes the same authority with which He lived and ministered available to us through His ongoing presence. "Jesus came and told his disciples, "I have been given all authority in heaven and on earth. Therefore, go and make disciples of all the nations, baptizing them in the name of the Father and the Son and the Holy Spirit. Teach these new disciples to obey all the commands I have given you. And be sure of this: I am with you always, even to the end of the age." (Matthew 28:18-20, NLT). So, biblically we have what it takes to bear fruit. What we need to do is consider what Jesus would be doing in our historical and cultural context if He were here today. He is here today, through us.

The answer is still a bit elusive, so perhaps we can consider different possibilities. Would Jesus hold large healing crusades, or would He visit people in hospitals and pray with them? Perhaps He would do both. Would Jesus give money to organizations that feed the poor, or would Jesus feed the poor? How would Jesus minister to the homeless? How would He go about loving members of youth gangs, and those entrapped in the drug culture? How would He reach out to the young woman considering an abortion, or show His compassion to a woman who just had one? What would He do or say if He happened to be downtown on the day of the Gay Pride parade? How would He show His love to single moms and their children? These are groups within our society that quickly come to mind. But what about the seemingly comfortable middle-class family? Perhaps, within those families women and children are being physically or sexually abused, just as they may be in any segment of society. They may be dealing with lost loved ones, or with serious marital issues. How would Jesus reach out to them? What about the wealthy that seems to have everything anyone could ever ask for, but are obviously not yet satisfied with life? These are often forgotten groups in the church's efforts to bear fruit.

This very list of questions highlights a problem. We tend to compartmentalize our society, and categorize people. Jesus didn't view people as belonging to certain groups or sub cultures. He viewed them as individuals who needed love, compassion, and perhaps, a miracle. They needed the miracle of salvation at the very least. They needed the miracle of salvation at the very most. We label people. We determine which group they belong to, and if we are really concerned, we send that group $20.00 a month so that they can help 'people like that'. Jesus ministered to individuals as individuals and touched their lives with His honest concern, His unconditional love, His power, and His saving grace. If every Christian did that, many of the Para-church ministries that we have today wouldn't need to exist. Sick persons would be prayed for individually by their Christian friend or neighbour. Drug addicts would have a Christian friend walking alongside them, helping them have a godly view of themselves. They could start to see themselves as having great value to God and society, and with God's help get clean. Youth gang members would have a Christian teenager befriending them and inviting them out to their youth group. Pregnant teens would have a gentle arm around them, encouraging them, teaching them, and presenting options to abortion. You get the idea. Every person in our community is an individual needing to experience the love of God individually. Most of the groups that work with specific segments of our society do an awesome job. They deserve our prayer and our support. But nothing can replace real one on one relationship with a loving and Christ-like believer. People need to hear the truth of God's Word in combination with sincere love and compassion. They need the miracle of salvation presented to them through life and word.

To attain this goal, we need every believer to set aside their pride, their inhibitions, and their shame in order to reveal the love and power of God to individuals. We need every believer to commit themselves to righteousness, so that people can see the joy and fulfilment of a life that is right before God. We need every believer to bear the fruit of the Spirit; or the fruit of Christ's character, so that people see the true nature of God and are drawn to Him.

Giving money to Para church organizations is a good thing. But your $20.00 bill can only go so far in revealing the love of Jesus. It can't smile at anyone. It can't give a lonely, hurting individual a hug. It can't hold someone's hand. It can't put an arm on someone's shoulder while praying for them. The people working and volunteering at most of these organizations are amazing people who do an amazing job. Just imagine, however, if every individual in the church took it upon him or herself to be Jesus to one person or family in need of Christ's love. Jesus, incarnate through His church, would change the world dramatically once again.

4 DONNING THE WHITE COAT

At the time of writing my son is in first year medical school. Early in the year there was what is labelled a "White Coat Ceremony". It was a wonderful, formal event that was akin to a graduation ceremony. The difference was that the students were graduating into the medical program, not out of it. It was here that prospective doctors were presented with their first white coat. I was extremely proud when my son's name was called out. He quickly appeared, walking across the stage with the white coat draped over his arm. He stopped half way across the stage. At that point a high-ranking school official took the coat from off his arm and put it on him. He then shook the hands of a few more platform guests and posed for official pictures. It all sounds quite formal. It was. It was also a moving experience to me for more than one reason.

God spoke truth to me that night. To me, the event was a church service as much as it was a meaningful ceremony. God was the preacher. I was the congregation. The sermon began even before the ceremony started. Having arrived early, I found myself looking through the brochure given us at the door. For the most part it was filled with names and credits of people I knew nothing about. But there was one portion that seemed to actually say something. I expected to find something in the brochure that I would read but never care to remember.

I was wrong: "The white coats our students will receive today bear the crest of the Medical DeGroote School of Medicine. It is my sincere hope that those who wear the coats will represent the values that the Faculty of Health Sciences holds true: excellence, accountability, integrity, respect, optimism, interdisciplinary collaboration and commitment to our communities." Immediately God began to speak to me. The truth of Isaiah 61:10 began to fill my mind and heart. "I am overwhelmed with joy in the LORD my God! For he has dressed me with the clothing of salvation and draped me in a robe of righteousness." (Isaiah 61:10, NLT). I began to think about the responsibility that accompanied the garment of salvation and the robe of righteousness. I thought about the importance of living excellent Christian lives. I thought about how we needed to live lives of integrity, and the importance of having respect for all of God's creation. The word "optimism" translated into "faith" in my present way of thinking. Interdisciplinary collaboration spoke to me about the magnitude that the teaching on the church functioning as a body has for us today. I thought about the commitment that the collective church must make to our communities.

As I pondered what the Spirit of God was speaking to me, we waited. We waited. We waited some more for 183 potential doctors to enter the room. It was 15 minutes past start time. It was as if we were in this giant waiting room at the doctor's office, and it was well past the appointed time. I leaned to my wife and said: "They should put a message on the screen: 'Get used to it'".

The large congregation stood in admiration as the students marched in. After respectful applause we were seated. Dr. John Kelton, Dean and Vice President,

Faculty of Health Sciences, began to speak. He was also the author of the comment referred to in the brochure. Through the course of his speech, he said three things that jumped out at me. I didn't have pen and paper, so a paraphrase will have to suffice. Dr. Kelton told the students, at this very significant moment in their lives, that this is not a time to celebrate. Celebration will come later. This is a time to take on the responsibility of becoming the best you can be. A truth was driven into my heart. Second, he said that we can't help everyone we have the opportunity to serve. But we do have the potential to harm everyone. Once again, I was impacted by this. Finally, he quoted Dr. William Osler. "Medicine is learned by the bedside and not in the classroom. Let not your conceptions of disease come from words heard in the lecture room or read from the book. See, and then reason and compare and control. But see first."

That evening was all about the fruit of righteousness to me. It was all about how we represent Jesus in our community. It was about the responsibility we take on ourselves the moment we put on the garment of salvation, or the robe of Christ's righteousness.

Celebration Comes Later

There was certainly a celebratory feel in the air that night. It was a proud event. You could feel excitement and see the positive anticipation of what lie before them on the students' faces. Pride oozed from parents, spouses, girlfriends, boyfriends, brothers and sisters. But it was made clear to all that this was not a time to celebrate. Celebration would come later. This is a time for work. There will be years of intense study. There will be internship and residency to follow. As much as joy and anticipation was appropriate, real celebration would have to wait for the work to be done.

The comparison to our Christianity is easy. There is a strong element of joy in our life with Christ now. We are told in Scripture to express that joy. "Always be full of joy in the Lord. I say it again—rejoice!" (Philippians 4:4, NLT). We are in the program! We now know who we are in Christ. We have been given our garment of salvation, our robe of righteousness. We have every right to be proud of our white coats. It is right and good for us to be thrilled with our new position in Christ. But there is so much to be done.

A huge celebration is coming. Jesus has gone to prepare a place for us, and when we get to heaven there will be a huge party at my mansion. You are invited. But for now there are other priorities.

Listen to how Jesus addressed this struggle. He had been performing great miracles in Galilee. He healed a leper. The Roman centurion's servant had been healed at Jesus' word, even though the servant was at some distant location. Jesus healed the disciple Peter's mother-in-law, which tells us that he was on the northern coast of the Sea of Galilee in Capernaum. Evening came, and many who were possessed by demons were brought to Jesus. He delivered them all. The sick were brought to Him. The Bible says that He healed every last one of them. What a time of celebration! Unbelievable excitement must have filled the air with each miracle. Even a Pharisee came to Jesus, excited about the possibility of serving Him. This was one of the religious leaders in Israel that typically hated Jesus and tried hard to prove His fallibility. Not this one; at least not now. He would follow Jesus anywhere. He wasn't alone either. There were others who were willing to leave everything behind them for the privilege of serving a man who spoke and ministered with such authority. Here is how Jesus responded: "Then one of the teachers of religious law said to him, "Teacher, I will follow you wherever you go." But Jesus replied, "Foxes have dens to live in, and birds have nests, but the Son of Man has no place even to lay his head." Another of his disciples said, "Lord, first let me return home and bury my father." But Jesus told him, "Follow me now. Let the spiritually dead bury their own dead." (Matthew 8:19-22, NLT)/ There is another story about a young man who had significant wealth. He wanted a white coat. He wanted to know how to enter the kingdom of God. Jesus told him to obey the commandments. He said that he did, but something was still missing. "Jesus answered, "If you want to be perfect, go, sell your possessions and give to the poor, and you will have treasure in heaven. Then come, follow me." When the young man heard this, he went away sad, because he had great wealth. Then Jesus said to his disciples, "I tell you the truth, it is hard for a rich man to enter the kingdom of heaven. Again, I tell you, it is easier for a camel to go through the eye of a needle than for a rich man to enter the kingdom of God." (Matthew 19:21-24, NIV).

We only have a partial understanding of what it means to bear the fruit of righteousness. It is not just about obeying the rules. Oh, living right is certainly part of righteousness. Let us not lose sight of the fact that righteousness is also about serving Jesus no matter what the cost.

If we are going to be effective fruit bearers, celebration is not our greatest priority right now. Neither are our homes. Neither is gaining riches, our retirement funds, or even things that we consider to be normal activities in life. A big part of righteousness is having right priorities for the time in which we live. Here they are:

- Know the Word of God so that you can live accordingly and so you can lead others to the truth
- Be the salt of the earth
- Be the light of the world
- Love your enemies and pray for those who persecute you
- Bless those who curse you
- Pray for those who mistreat you
- Turn the other cheek
- Give to everyone who asks, and expect nothing back
- Treat others as you would like to be treated
- Be good to your enemies
- Don't judge others or you will be judged
- Forgive and you will be forgiven
- Give and it will be given to you
- If you see someone that is hungry, give them something to eat
- If someone is thirsty, give them something to drink
- If someone needs clothes, clothe them
- If someone is sick, look after them
- If someone is in prison, visit them
- Don't worry about stuff. Seek God's kingdom and His righteousness first and know that the things you need for life will be given to you
- Be holy as God is holy

Jesus taught all these things. These are the fruit of His righteousness in us. It was and is so easy to let these truths go in one ear and out the other, while getting all excited about the things Jesus does for us. There is too much "righteous" work to do to get trapped in the place of celebration.

Rejoice at the donning of the white coat. Be thankful for your garment of salvation and the robe of Christ's righteousness. Then get to work! The real celebration has to wait. Now is a time of preparation. Now is a time of sharing. Now is a time to bring Jesus to the world. Now is the time to bear the fruit of Christ's righteousness.

The Potential to Harm

Dr. Kelton spoke of when hospitals were first developed in the city of Hamilton, Ontario, Canada. The first permanent hospital opened in the early 1850's. Doctors wore white coats in the hospital to identify themselves as people who were there to help. He spoke of a time in history when people were mysteriously getting ill in hospitals. Some were even dying. The only common denominator in the hospital was the presence of doctors. A reasonable deduction seemed to be that perhaps the cause of the illness had something to do with the doctors themselves.

If bacteria had been discovered, it was not yet fully understood. Someone decided that perhaps it was the doctors that were potentially causing harm. It was determined that they should wash their hands more regularly. The deadly illnesses decreased and finally disappeared. The doctors, identified with white coats as people there to help, were harming the patients because they weren't clean enough. My mind went to Dr. Kelton's earlier statement that "we can't help everyone we have opportunity to serve. But we do have the potential to harm everyone." My thoughts then bolted into the Psalms. "Who may climb the mountain of the LORD? Who may stand in his holy place? Only those whose hands and hearts are pure." (Psalms 24:3-4, NLT).

This is such an important statement about living a life that bears godly fruit. If we do not bear the fruit of righteousness, we are causing harm to the kingdom of God. If we, as people wearing robes of Christ's righteousness, are harbouring sin we are harming rather than helping those around us in their spiritual journey. We are not only fruitless; we are carriers of disease. Avoid sin at all costs. Keep your hands clean. Sin is a communicable disease that can easily become a plague spread by people with white robes. It keeps us from greater intimacy with God, and it hurts others.

If there is sin in our lives, two very negative things happen to those who know us best. They may be our children, our brothers and sisters, our workmates, or our best friends. First, they will come to believe that sin is normal and acceptable. Second, they will not see it as harmful. Because you do it, they will honestly believe that they can engage in ungodly activity without it damaging their relationship to God and others. Our Christianity will not stand out as a better way of living because they don't see it as a different way of living. The only thing different about Christianity to them is that the Christian goes to church meetings. The greatest danger is for people to believe that they can put faith in God unto salvation, and that such faith doesn't require any change from them.

The inversion of this truth is wonderful. When we keep our hands clean we can have a sanctifying effect on our society. The more 'clean' there is in society, the healthier it is. Clean becomes the norm. For example: If the majority of people in a community are against abortion, there would be fewer abortions. If there are not enough people in a community that would support a strip club, there would be no strip club. Cleanliness begets cleanliness.

A second reality is that even those in secular society behave differently around holy people than they do around unholy people. If you are a Christian who keeps your robe of righteousness clean, you have probably experienced this. A person often cleans up their language, refrains from telling off colour jokes, and generally behaves differently. The truth is that most people in our society have an inherent respect for holiness. Some Christians demand this. They demand the unbeliever to talk and behave differently around them because they are Christians, and yet they gossip and judge their fellow employees constantly. Note this: the doctor with the white coat can't point a finger at the patient and demand that they get better when the doctor himself has carried sickness into the hospital. Your responsibility is to keep your white robe clean, not to endeavour to clean others before they have received the garment of salvation. It is unreasonable to expect people who do not have Christ in their hearts to live as if they do. Trying to legislate that is pointless. On the other hand, understand that your holiness will affect the way they live. The prayer would be that they see the beauty of the sin free life and decide that it is what they want for themselves. Then you can offer Jesus and the garment of salvation to them. Your fruit of righteousness has then born the fruit of salvation.

Another important insight is that holy people create an atmosphere in which the Holy Spirit can move and impact the lives of others. When there is no conflict between the message you share and the life you live, you have provided a powerful tool for God to use. The only obstruction between God and the unsaved is in the heart and mind of the hearer. If the white robes of believers are unsoiled, the Holy Spirit can break through those barriers much easier than if our robes are dirty. Our hypocrisy is often the spiritual bacteria that prevent effective propagation of the Gospel message.

Here are some great Scriptural directives on how to keep our robes clean. "Avoid worthless, foolish talk that only leads to more godless behavior. This kind of talk spreads like cancer" (2 Timothy 2:16-17, NLT). Note the medical reference. Foolish talk spreads like a deadly disease. "Let there be no sexual immorality, impurity, or greed among you. Such sins have no place among God's people. Obscene stories, foolish talk, and coarse jokes—these are not for you. Instead, let there be thankfulness to God. You can be sure that no immoral, impure, or greedy person will inherit the Kingdom of Christ and of God. For a greedy person is an idolater, worshiping the things of this world." (Ephesians 5:3-5, NLT) "For once you were full of darkness, but now you have light from the Lord. So live as people of light! For this light within you produces only what is good and right and true. Carefully determine what pleases the Lord. Take no part in the worthless deeds of evil and darkness; instead, expose them. It is shameful even to talk about the things that ungodly people do in secret." (Ephesians 5:8-12, NLT). Here it is in a nutshell: "Test everything. Hold on to the good. Avoid every kind of evil." (1 Thessalonians 5:21-22, NIV)

If the Christian church is going to bring a cure for sin to a sin sick world, we must be free of infection ourselves. Sin is an infectious disease. It is contagious. We may not see it happening, but if we are carriers of sin it is affecting everyone around us. "We can't help everyone we have opportunity to serve. But we do have the potential to harm everyone."

Not everyone around us wants to hear the message we would like to share with them. That is their personal choice and freedom. However, everyone around us will be affected by the life we live.

By the Bedside

"Medicine is learned by the bedside and not in the classroom. Let not your conceptions of disease come from words heard in the lecture room or read from the book. See, and then reason and compare and control. But see first." (Dr. William Osler). This statement doesn't translate perfectly into our Christian context, but there is something very important to be learned here.

Our book, the Bible, is the most important educational tool we have as a church. Keep reading it! Our lecture room, the church, is better than any school. We meet the Holy Spirit there. In that context He can drive Biblical truth into our spirits and change us forever. Keep going to church! The comments about the lecture room or words from the book do not apply. Still, there is an amazing lesson in this comment.

There is nothing as wonderful as seeing the Gospel at work in the streets. When you take what you learn from God's Word and His Spirit, and then take that truth outside the four walls of the church, something incredible can happen. You find a sin sick soul. They may be rich or poor, well fed or hungry. No matter what their situation in life, they need Jesus. So, you share what you know, then watch as God does His healing work in their lives. You watch fear and confusion fall off of them. You watch as a sense of purpose fills their heart. You watch as hopelessness turns to faith, and fear turns to peace. What you learn at that moment is not learned sitting in the pew. A hundred sermons and Bible studies can't teach this. Your understanding of the power of the gospel is converted from intellectual understanding to absolute certainty, right there in the streets. What you see at the moment of their salvation is the most powerful lesson you will learn since your own experience of being born again. The excitement about serving Jesus that followed your own salvation is revitalized as you see fruit born at the bedside of your community.

Praying for someone in need and watching God answer prayer has a similar affect. Watching the alcoholic being set free from his or her addiction is amazing. Watching the drug addict being set free is life changing. Watching the sick or diseased being healed is truly incredible. These bedside events will change your life. They will convert intellectual faith into real and unshakeable faith.

The challenge is for you to actually wear your white coats into the streets. Make sure they are clean. Wash your hands. Put your education into practice, then reason and compare what you have learned with what you see. When you see God's truth and power impact the lives of others, it will take your faith and zeal in serving Jesus to a whole new height.

"I am overwhelmed with joy in the LORD my God! For he has dressed me with the clothing of salvation and draped me in a robe of righteousness." (Isaiah 61:10, NLT) That is enough to make us want to celebrate for sure. It is the garment of salvation and the robe of His righteousness that gives us the assurance of entry into our eternal and glorious home. Rejoice now, but the real celebration will have to wait. There is work to do, and a lot of it. We have graduated into the kingdom of God, but we have not yet graduated out of this world. As long as we are here we have a tremendous responsibility. The world around us is sin sick. Our cities are sin sick. Our communities are sin sick. Our neighbourhoods are sin sick. In some cases, our families are sin sick.

As we don our white coats and exit the church - as we walk through our individual world, we can help some, bearing godly fruit, or we can harm all. That is our choice. When our hands are clean and we take all that we know about God's grace, love, and power to the bedsides of our communities, we will see the healing that such grace, love, and power can truly bring. We will see godly fruit, only enhancing the excitement of our coming celebration. On that day of graduation and celebration, we will be presented with a crown to complement our white robe. How exciting! "And now the prize awaits me—the crown of righteousness, which the Lord, the righteous Judge, will give me on the day of his return. And the prize is not just for me but for all who eagerly look forward to his appearing." (2 Timothy 4:8, NLT).

5 A PURPOSEFUL ANOINTING

When I was a child, Samson was one of those Bible heroes that captivated my attention. When I heard the stories of his great feats, I was in awe. He was the Bible's Hercules. He was Scripture's Superman. The story of this man's strength filled my imagination until it was of comic book, super hero proportions. But it was all very real. Samson's life was supernatural right from the very beginning.

Judges 13 explains the supernatural circumstances of his birth. "In those days a man named Manoah from the tribe of Dan lived in the town of Zorah. His wife was unable to become pregnant, and they had no children. The angel of the LORD appeared to Manoah's wife and said, "Even though you have been unable to have children, you will soon become pregnant and give birth to a son." (Judges 13:2-3, NLT) Samson was born to a sterile woman, and his birth was announced by the Angel of the Lord before he was even conceived. At the announcement of Samson's conception the prospective parents offered a burnt offering to the Lord. Now allow yourself to imagine this: as the flame blazed high into the sky, the angel of the Lord stepped into the fire and ascended heavenward in the flame (Judges 13:20). How amazing must that have been? Samson's existence was surrounded by the supernatural from the very beginning.

From the very moment of conception, Samson was to be set apart from the normal stream of society. He would be different from the other kids at school. Samson would not be like the other guys at work. The Nazirite vow was typically a male act of commitment made to the Lord for a specific period of time, like a fast. The word Nazirite means "separated" or "dedicated". With Samson, however, even his mother had to live by the strict regulations of the vow from the moment of conception until his birth. Samson's life was to be separated unto the Lord for his entire lifetime. His life was to be dedicated to God from beginning to end. He was to be set apart for supernatural purposes.

The vow itself was quite simple, if done for a relatively short period. He was to drink no wine or vinegar. There would be no grape juice, grapes, or raisins. No razor was ever to touch his head and his hair was to never be cut. He couldn't go near a dead body, even if it was his mother or father who passed away. Over a life time, this was quite a commitment.

Samson was not just set apart from these things. Samson was set apart to something. His supernatural birth and unusual lifestyle was because he was set apart for a unique purpose. "You will become pregnant and give birth to a son, and his hair must never be cut. For he will be dedicated to God as a Nazirite from birth. He will begin to rescue Israel from the Philistines." (Judges 13:5, NLT),

As a child, in my imagination, everything about Samson was supernatural. He seemed like a man who lived a life that was beyond normal. I was wrong. As I grew to a fuller understanding about Samson's life, I became less enthralled. I recognized that a severe contradiction existed. Here was a man who lived according to a strict creed in order to fulfil his special place in the purposes of God. He killed a lion with his bare hands, took on thirty men at one time, and killed a thousand men single-handedly in one battle. At the same time, he lied habitually. He was attracted to a Philistine woman whom some think to have been a prostitute, and yet, he continued to expect and experience God's blessing.

The question that haunts us about Samson's life is important, because we may struggle with contradictions in our own lives. When you assess your own spiritual life, you mean it quite seriously when you say that you desire to serve Him wholeheartedly. Your commitment to Him is real, but there are contradictions. There are periods of great spiritual blessings, and there are periods of significant spiritual weakness. There are times when God uses you powerfully, all the while knowing that there is sin in your life.

You can identify with Samson on more than one level. You have been born both naturally and supernaturally. You are born again by the Spirit of God. "This means that anyone who belongs to Christ has become a new person. The old life is gone; a new life has begun!" (2 Corinthians 5:17, NLT). It is a supernatural life that begins with supernatural rebirth. Not only that, we are called to a consecrated life. "Therefore, come out from among unbelievers, and separate yourselves from them, says the LORD. Don't touch their filthy things, and I will welcome you." (2 Corinthians 6:17, NLT). You also have a defined purpose. "So we are Christ's ambassadors; God is making his appeal through us. We speak for Christ when we plead, "Come back to God!" (2 Corinthians 5:20, NLT). We are to be ministers of reconciliation to a world that is separated from God. To accomplish this we are to be people of the Spirit; anointed by God. His power is at work in us to do mighty things to fulfil His purpose for His glory. Jesus said that we, the church, will do even greater things than He did. "I tell you the truth, anyone who believes in me will do the same works I have done, and even greater works, because I am going to be with the Father. You can ask for anything in my name, and I will do it, so that the Son can bring glory to the Father." (John 14:12-1, NLT). But we have a problem! We have attachments to things that belong to the enemy. We are often attracted to things that would cause us to commit spiritual adultery, offending God as our first love. There are times when God uses us, and there are other times when we seem to be devoid of His power.

It is essential that we deal with the questions about Samson's life honestly, and learn something about his life that will help us become what God wants us to be – consistently. We must come to grips with this conflict within ourselves in order that we can resolve it and accomplish all that He has set out for us to do – to bear fruit consistently.

Anointing Abuse

When I compare the church that I see in most locations today to the church I read about in Acts chapters 2 through 10, I struggle to find comparison. I once heard a preacher say that "If the purpose of the thing is not known, to abuse it is inevitable." Is it possible that we as a church have forgotten why we exist? Is it possible that we have lost sight of the fact that our primary purpose is to bear godly fruit? There is no doubt that the Holy Spirit is moving today. Certainly, He is filling, baptizing, and empowering believers just as He did in the days of old. Christians are being healed. Christians flock to altars where they are being blessed. Many evidences of the Holy Spirit's presence are apparent at Christian gatherings. The problem is that most of these evidences of the presence of God are happening inside church walls. Few or no unbelievers are present at these gatherings. As a result, the church is not being added to daily as it was in its early days. In fact, in most local churches, they are not being added to weekly, monthly, or even yearly. We have lost sight of the fact that the power of the Holy Spirit is intended to be power to witness. We seem to have forgotten that the miracles take place to confirm God's Word and would be most effective outside the church where the gospel is being preached. Healings and miracles are not just for believers. Gone are the days when Christians believe that the greatest manifestation of the Holy Spirit is righteous living, bearing the nine-fold fruit of the Holy Spirit, and power to share the good news about Jesus. There is a feeling that the power of God is available to us to have great services with various manifestations of God's Spirit blessing His people. We have forgotten why we exist; therefore, abuse of the anointing is inevitable. It is this very problem that leads to the fulfilment of the Apostle Paul's prophecy regarding the nature of the church in the last days: "They will act religious, but they will reject the power that could make them godly." (2 Timothy 3:5, NLT)

Samson's purpose was singular. He was to begin the deliverance of Israel from the Philistine nation (Judges 13:5). When he was committed to fulfilling that purpose, he had great power. When he busied himself doing other things he was a weak human being. Within his purpose

Samson faced various challenges.

Samson killed a lion with his bare hands! For the animal rights people out there, it was self-defense. He was simply walking along the road, on his way to meet a Philistine woman who would become his wife. This may seem strange, but it was okay. This was a marriage ordained by God. This would be the beginning of Samson's involvement with the Philistine people. His marriage would provide an opportunity for Samson to confront Israel's oppressors. As he and his parents were on their way to Timnah, a young lion came roaring toward him, seemingly out of nowhere. This could have been the end of Samson right then and there. Instead, the Scripture records that "At that moment the Spirit of the LORD came powerfully upon him, and he ripped the lion's jaws apart with his bare hands. He did it as easily as if it were a young goat. But he didn't tell his father or mother about it." (Judges 14:6, NLT). Defeating the lion fell within the boundaries of his purpose. After all, if he died on the way to Timnah he never would have had opportunity to fulfil his Divine purpose. So, God's Spirit came upon him in power, giving him supernatural ability to tear that lion apart with his bare hands. The Apostle Peter offers us this stern warning: "Stay alert! Watch out for your great enemy, the devil. He prowls around like a roaring lion, looking for someone to devour." (1 Peter 5:8, NLT). Know this: Satan will do everything he can to prevent you from fulfilling your purpose. He will attempt to destroy you before you even get started. And if that is unsuccessful, he will attempt to distract you once you do. But, there is a power available to you. As certain as Peter's warning may be, it is equally certain that "the Spirit who lives in you is greater than the spirit who lives in the world." (1 John 4:4, NLT). Defeating him is part of your purpose. He will do everything in his power to prevent you from being a fruit bearer. He will do everything in his power to cause you to bear unrighteous fruit by tempting you to sin. He will attempt to replace the fruit of the Holy Spirit with a judgmental attitude, depression, worry, impatience, a harsh attitude toward others, etc. It is easy to see that if you are living that kind of life it is impossible to bear godly fruit. It is impossible to be Christ's ambassador. You will not be successful in evangelism. In fact it is unlikely that you will even try. If you want to be a successful fruit bearer you will deal with the devil. There is Divine power available to do so.

Samson's new wife betrayed him on the last day of their seven day wedding feast. Samson didn't have any Philistine friends to hang out with at this week-long celebration, so he was assigned thirty of them. He begins this relationship by giving them a riddle. The arrangement was that if they could figure out the answer to the riddle by the end of the seven days, he would give each of them a linen garment and a set of clothing. If they couldn't figure out the riddle, they would each give Samson a linen garment and a set of clothes. The thirty men soon realized the difficulty of the riddle, and began hounding Samson's new wife for the answer. She didn't know, but appealed to Samson every day for him to reveal it to her. Finally, on the last day of the wedding week, Samson told her. She, in turn, revealed the answer to the Philistine men. And so it begins. Samson's confrontation with the Philistine people would start right here. The Spirit of the Lord came upon him in power. He marched himself down to the Philistine city of Ashkelon, struck down thirty men, and took their belongings – including their clothes. The clothes were given to his wedding companions. Unknown to him, his wife was given to the wedding attendant, likely to have been one of the thirty.

Samson was a little upset when he found out that his wife had been given away to someone else. He took it out on the Philistines by catching three hundred foxes. He tied their tails together in pairs, fastened a torch to each pair of tails, lit the torch, and let the foxes loose in the grain fields, vineyards, and olive groves. The Philistines seemed to take offense to this. When they discovered who caused such havoc and cost to their crops they killed Samson's former wife and her father. Samson was irate. He attacked the Philistines and killed many of them. An army of Philistine soldiers was sent to Judah to find Samson. The Philistines wanted him dead. Now Samson's own people, who were currently Philistine subjects, felt very threatened. Three thousand Israelite soldiers tracked Samson down in order to hand him over to the Philistines. They would most certainly kill him. Samson confidently agreed to be bound with ropes and go quietly. The Philistines were delighted when they saw Samson's own people delivering him to them. They ran toward him with loud shouts of victory. The Scripture records: "But the Spirit of the LORD came powerfully upon Samson, and he snapped the ropes on his arms as if they were burnt strands of flax, and they fell from his wrists. Then he found the jawbone of a recently killed donkey. He picked it up and killed 1,000 Philistines with it." (Judges 15:14-15, NLT). Every time Samson confronted his purpose, to begin the deliverance of Israel from the people of Philistia, the Spirit of the Lord came upon him in power.

If the purpose of the church is to "Go into all the

world and preach the Good News to everyone" (Mark 16:15, NLT) then we can expect the anointing of God to be released in us when we commit ourselves to that end. We are ministers of reconciliation. We are ambassadors of Christ. Our function is to bring to the world what Christ made available to all of us on the cross of Calvary. "If the purpose of the thing is not known, to abuse it is inevitable." We have abused Christ's anointing by forgetting our purpose as a church. We have enjoyed His power and His presence in our services, and so we should. We have prayed for sick and needy Christians within our church families, and so we should. We have counselled brothers and sisters in Christ that need direction. We have done it all with the anointing of God on our lives, but we are not using it for the main purpose for which it is given. How much longer can we expect the power of God to be poured out on the church if we are simply going to bask in it rather than use it for His purposes, and to bear godly fruit?

We often mistake renewal as revival. We get stuck there. We are blessed by it. If renewal does not progress to revival, it would be like Samson experiencing the Spirit of the Lord coming upon him in power, sitting down, and proclaiming: "What a rush!" but doing nothing to confront his purpose. What a waste that would be! Real historical revivals resulted in large numbers of people finding Christ, because people went beyond renewal and used the power of the Holy Spirit for the purpose for which we were given supernatural birth – to be fruit bearers.

Within the overall purpose of bearing the fruit of souls, there are many tasks. There are numerous functions. You have a specific place within the body of

Christ. God has a specific will for your life that fits within the overall purpose of the church. You have a responsibility to find that place. You have a responsibility to prepare yourself to do the work God has called you to do, and you have a responsibility to do it without ever losing sight of the overall purpose. The anointing is not about you. It is about them. It is for the purpose of bearing godly fruit. When we get that right, we can expect God's anointing to be stirred up within us for the task He places before us.

There are some powerful New Testament examples of this.

Peter's Powerful Proclamation

In the book of Matthew, chapter 10, Jesus was sending out the twelve disciples to do some ministry. In the passage He promises this: "When you are arrested, don't worry about how to respond or what to say. God will give you the right words at the right time. For it is not you who will be speaking—it will be the Spirit of your Father speaking through you." (Matthew 10:19-20, NLT). Peter was one of those twelve. He is often referred to as impetuous Peter because he had a habit of doing and saying things without thinking it through. That wasn't always a bad thing. After all, he was the only one of the twelve that walked on water because he acted in faith without letting his mind get in the way – at least for a minute or two.

On the other hand, his impetuous nature sometimes got him in trouble. On one occasion, Jesus was prophesying His coming death and resurrection. Peter actually rebuked Jesus for saying such things. Jesus' response was quick and seemingly harsh: "Get away from me, Satan!" he said. "You are seeing things merely from a human point of view, not from God's." (Mark 8:33, NLT).

It was Peter who had the not-so-brilliant idea of erecting three tents on the Mount of Transfiguration; one for Jesus, one for Moses, and one for Elijah. He completely misunderstood what this amazing event was all about, and was ignoring the fact that Jesus had to die and be resurrected before the fullness of His glory could be seen.

It was this same disciple who claimed that he would never stumble in His commitment to Jesus. Shortly thereafter he openly denied knowing Christ three times after Jesus' arrest. Fear controlled this bold follower of Christ. So it is well established that Peter, the disciple, was often impulsive and even weak.

On the day of Pentecost, as recorded in Acts 2, Peter was different. There were thousands of people present in the temple courts that day, many of which had shouted: "Crucify Him! Crucify Him!" at Jesus' unfair trial. The Holy Spirit had fallen on the disciples in an unusual manner on this day. Peter had a purpose, and Peter had power. This same man, who had denied even know Christ just fifty-three days before, now stood before the massive crowd. Under the anointing of the Holy Spirit, he told the story of Jesus, and three thousand souls were won for the kingdom of God that day. He committed to his purpose. The anointing was released through Him. Fruit was plentiful. That is how it works.

This same Peter preached the gospel at Cornelius' house soon after. As a Jew, he should never have entered the house of a Gentile. In this case it was his purpose. God told him to go. When he preached Christ and Christ crucified, the power of God fell and they were all baptized in the Holy Spirit.

Stephen's Superior Show of Power

Stephen was one of the first seven elected church elders. He was a man that was full of God's grace and power. Through him God did great wonders and miraculous signs. It was annoying! At least to the leaders of the Jewish synagogue it was. So they chose to do what any good religious leader would do. Kill him! Stephen preached a great sermon, proving why Jesus was their long-awaited Messiah. Unfortunately, this statement seemed to upset them a little: You stubborn people! You are heathen at heart and deaf to the truth. Must you forever resist the Holy Spirit? That's what your ancestors did, and so do you!" (Acts 7:51, NLT). They didn't take it well. "When they heard this, they were furious and gnashed their teeth at him." (Acts 7:54, NIV). In our brief historical record of Stephen and his ministry, this statement is recorded: "they could not stand up against his wisdom or the Spirit by whom he spoke." (Acts 6:10, NIV) I love the balance of maturity and spirituality in Stephen. The only means of quieting the anointing on his life to do the work of Christ was to kill him. Stephen was continually committed to his purpose, and continually confounded the wise because of the rich anointing being released through Him.

Philip's Private Meeting

Philip was another one of the original seven elders. He was ministering in Samaria and experiencing great revival. Miracles were taking place. People were getting saved. But God had a different purpose for Philip. "As for

Philip, an angel of the Lord said to him, "Go south down the desert road that runs from Jerusalem to Gaza." So he started out, and he met the treasurer of Ethiopia, a eunuch of great authority under the Kandake, the queen of Ethiopia. The eunuch had gone to Jerusalem to worship, and he was now returning. Seated in his carriage, he was reading aloud from the book of the prophet Isaiah. The Holy Spirit said to Philip, "Go over and walk along beside the carriage." (Acts 8:26-29, NLT). At this particular time, Philip's purpose was not the masses. It was one man. He ministered with the anointing of God and this one man became the first missionary to Ethiopia. He committed to fulfilling his purpose and the anointing was released to touch the heart of the eunuch. Who knows how many came to know Jesus as a result of this one man's efforts in the African country? When you forget what your purpose is you either lose or abuse the anointing. It is essential that you know your function within the body of Christ. That place can be one of many things, but the ultimate end will be to help the body of Christ be effective in the fulfilment of the great commission. It is when you find your place in the body, and commit to it, that the anointing is released in you to bear fruit. If you don't do this, your Christianity will tend to become selfish and ingrown. It is often then that Christians struggle in their lifestyle which begins to conflict with their testimony. It is true that if the purpose of the anointing is not known, or forgotten, to abuse it is inevitable.

Where Does it all Come From?

We tend to treat the anointing as something God gives us for the moment, and then it is gone. It may have been that way in Samson's day, but we live in a different spiritual economy. Here is how it works in a nutshell: The anointing belongs to Jesus; Jesus lives in us by His Holy Spirit, and His anointing is released through us when we stay committed to fulfilling the purposes He has for our lives.

Biblical support for this concept is easy to find. To do so, let's track a few events in the life of Jesus. After being baptized in water by John the Baptist, Jesus was led by the Holy Spirit to go into the dessert mountains to fast for forty days. During that time He was tempted by Satan himself. He came out of that place of testing totally victorious. Now thirty years old, He was ready to start His ministry. He was filled with the Spirit's power. He regularly taught in the synagogues with great authority, and word about Him began to spread. He soon found His way to His boyhood home, the city of Nazareth. Once again, Jesus stood up to read the Scriptures. The scroll written by the prophet Isaiah was handed to Him. He opens it to what we know of as Isaiah 61:1-2. "The Spirit of the Sovereign LORD is upon me, for the LORD has anointed me to bring good news to the poor. He has sent me to comfort the brokenhearted and to proclaim that captives will be released and prisoners will be freed. He has sent me to tell those who mourn that the time of the LORD's favor has come, and with it, the day of God's anger against their enemies." (Isaiah 61:1-2, NLT). He looked into the congregation and said: "The Scripture you've just heard has been fulfilled this very day!" (Luke 4:21, NLT).

Two things are very clear. First, Jesus claimed to be the anointed one, the one prophesied about by the great prophet Isaiah. We often refer to Him as 'Jesus Christ'. 'Christ' is not His last name. It is more like a title. The Greek word is 'Christos', which means 'anointed'.

When we say 'Jesus Christ' we are actually saying 'Jesus the anointed'. After Jesus quizzed his disciples about who people were saying He was, He asked them: "But who do you say I am?" Peter responded: "You are the Messiah, the Son of the living God." Jesus replied, "You are blessed, Simon son of John, because my Father in heaven has revealed this to you. You did not learn this from any human being." (Matthew 16:16-17, NLT). Jesus accepted the label of Messiah, which is the Hebrew equivalent of the word Christ. It was a truth revealed to Peter by the Heavenly Father Himself. Jesus is the Anointed One ...period! Jesus is His Name. Christ is His position. The anointing belongs to Jesus. It is not our anointing, it is His.

The second thing we learn from the passage in Isaiah is the purpose of the anointing. It is to preach the Gospel, to help the hurting, to set the people free from sin, and to let the people know that the day of the Lord's favour has come.

When you became a Christian, something amazing happened. The Apostle Paul asked the Corinthian Christians: "Don't you know that you yourselves are God's temple and that God's Spirit lives in you?" (1 Corinthians 3:16, NIV). The anointing that we talk about is Christ's anointing, who dwells in us by His Holy Spirit. The Apostle John says it plainly: "But you have an anointing from the Holy One, and all of you know the truth." (1 John 2:20, NIV). A few verses later he wrote: "As for you, the anointing you received from him remains in you, and you do not need anyone to teach you. But as his anointing teaches you about all things and as that anointing is real, not counterfeit—just as it has taught you, remain in him." (1 John 2:27, NIV). We don't need to ask

God for the anointing. We don't need to face every ministry opportunity wondering if God will give us the anointing. We don't need to fear that God will leave us powerless. If we are Christians, we have the anointing. Our concern is to bear the fruit of righteousness, and commit to fulfilling our purpose – which is so clearly defined in Isaiah 61:1-2.

Jesus said that: "Whoever believes in me, as the Scripture has said, streams of living water will flow from within him." (John 7:38, NIV). The Greek word that is translated "within him" is 'koilia'. It is the word for womb or belly. We are like the womb of God or belly of God. In us are streams of living water. We are not the source of those streams, but we are the carrier. We cannot produce life, but Christ's life can flow out of us. That is the anointing! And when we commit to fulfilling our purpose, it allows the anointing of Christ to be released through us. Then we will bear godly fruit for His glory.

There are often contradictions in our lives. They blockade the anointing from flowing through us. A contradiction is a contrast between who we claim to be when we call ourselves Christians and who we appear to be to those around us. These contradictions exist because we choose sin over sanctification. They are there because we live selfishly rather than selflessly. Where contradiction exists, godly fruit doesn't. However, when we commit ourselves to bearing the godly fruit of righteousness, our life and testimony will line up the way they should and Christ-like character will grow in us. Living out the character of Christ will lead to the salvation of souls.

The purpose of the anointing is ultimately so that the kingdom of God would grow, that individuals would come to know Jesus. That is our definitive purpose as a church. When our lives and testimony line up, when we bear the fruit of Christ's character, we can look that purpose in the eye with expectancy. We can expect that the Holy Spirit will come upon us in power to fulfil the role He has for us within the body of Christ. We can expect the anointing of Christ to be released in us to accomplish great feats for Him. We will have supernatural power to do supernatural things. We can expect souls to be won for the kingdom of God.

6 DEATH TO US ALL

In the horticultural world, death comes before life. Seeds have to die before life can spring up. In the realm of bearing godly fruit, death also comes first. Jesus said: "If you try to hang on to your life, you will lose it. But if you give up your life for my sake and for the sake of the Good News, you will save it." (Mark 8:35, NLT). Let's continue to look at the life of Samson. For this unusual man, dying to self was a long and difficult process that is most certainly enlightening. Yet, his death resulted in his most fruitful conquest.

Death to Selfish Desire

Sometime after the death of Samson's wife, he became interested in another Philistine woman. Her name was Delilah. Unlike his first marriage, a relationship with this Philistine woman was not of God. It was dangerous. It was risky. It was not consistent with God's will for Samson's life. Samson wasn't confronting the enemy; he was flirting with the enemy.

Judges 16 lists a series of attempts by Delilah to trick Samson. It would potentially be a very profitable venture for her. The rulers of the Philistines promised her 1000 pieces of silver from each of them if she could simply find the secret to Samson's strength. Each one of her devious attempts was followed by a lie from Samson in an attempt to protect himself. Although romantically involved with a woman of questionable character, and despite Samson's lies, he was given unusual strength to deliver himself from the enemy's attempts. Here is how it happened.

"Delilah said to Samson, 'Please tell me what makes you so strong and what it would take to tie you up securely.' Samson replied, "If I were tied up with seven new bowstrings that have not yet been dried, I would become as weak as anyone else." (Judges 16:6-7, NLT). The Philistine rulers got the necessary bowstrings and gave them to Delilah. She had some Philistine men lying in wait in another room in her house as she tied Samson up. She exclaimed to Samson that the Philistines had come to capture him. Without hesitation, Samson snapped the bowstrings off of him like a string snaps when burned by fire. An almost identical scenario takes place with brand new ropes. Remarkably, Samson broke them off of him as if they were thread. Delilah is beginning to lose patience with Samson's story-telling, but she makes a third attempt. Samson is becoming very creative with his lies. I can almost hear him chuckle to himself as he gives her this story. He tells Delilah that he will lose his strength if she weaves his hair into the fabric on her loom. So, when Samson goes to sleep, she does exactly that. Apparently, Samson is a sound sleeper. He never awoke until Delilah shouted the warning of fast approaching Philistines. Once again, he shows incredible strength by pulling his hair out of the loom, now woven into the fabric. Ouch!

One important thing to note here is that on each of these occasions there were Philistine men in the house. Samson's purpose was to confront the Philistines, but there is absolutely no record of him doing so. His purpose stared him in the face, and he did nothing about it. His lustful desires for Delilah derailed him. The fruit of righteousness was replaced by the fruit of selfish desire. This immature act caused him to lose complete site of the reason for which he was given supernatural birth. The fruit bearing life that flowed through him would not be sustained much longer without a complete turnaround.

If we have God's power but don't remain focused on God's purposes, we will abuse the power. That is what Samson was doing here. It was an immature use of God's anointing. In fact, it was an abuse of the strength God had given him. Samson wasn't unique in this. Some evangelists have sold miracles. Some ministers of the gospel have used the notoriety gained by their ministry to accumulate great wealth. It is not the wealth that is the concern. God will bless whom He chooses to bless. It is the misuse of notoriety that is the concern. Some men of God have used their position of fame and authority in ways that are abusive in their relationships with others. God is often very patient in waiting for us to do what we were given supernatural birth to do, but He is not patient with the abuse of His anointing. There is a passage of Scripture that speaks to this with startling clarity. "Not everyone who calls out to me, 'Lord! Lord!' will enter the Kingdom of Heaven. Only those who actually do the will of my Father in heaven will enter. On judgment day many will say to me, 'Lord! Lord! We prophesied in your name and cast out demons in your name and performed many miracles in your name.' But I will reply, 'I never knew you. Get away from me, you who break God's laws.'" (Matthew 7:21-23, NLT). Use of the anointing for anything other than God's purposes has no eternal value! Jesus said so.

As selfish desires took predominance in Samson's life it would eventually kill the life-giving, fruit-bearing anointing. We must die to selfish desires in order to be fruit producing Christians. The purposes of God must always take pre-eminence over personal longings.

Death to Temptation

Now Delilah was mad. She tried all of her wily ways. She pouted. "She tormented him with her nagging day after day until he was sick to death of it." (Judges 16:16, NLT). There is some good fodder for relationship counselling in this passage, but that is yet another subject. "Finally, Samson shared his secret with her. "My hair has never been cut," he confessed, "for I was dedicated to God as a Nazirite from birth. If my head were shaved, my strength would leave me, and I would become as weak as anyone else." (Judges 16:17, NLT). That was it! He had given in to temptation. The beans had been spilled. His relationship with unrighteousness became his downfall. The same set of events followed. This time, however, it ended differently. It was tragic. "When he woke up, he thought, "I will do as before and shake myself free." But he didn't realize the LORD had left him." (Judges 16:20, NLT) His strength was gone. The anointing left. If Samson was going to live for self, and not fulfil his godly purpose, then God would not continue to give Him the strength to do so. God had been far more tolerant with Samson than He needed to be, but now Samson had made a conscious decision to break his vow. He was rejecting God and rejecting the purpose for which he was given supernatural birth.

We must die to temptation in order to be fruit producing Christians. The flow of Christ's life giving, fruit bearing anointing through us directly relates to our determination to live righteous lives, or our lack thereof. When we put down or resist temptation of any type it allows for a greater flow of anointing through our lives.

Death to Temporal Values

There is another consideration in this as well. When we are too much like the world we cannot minister to the world. When the line of separation that divides those who follow Jesus from those that live for self gets too clouded, we cannot minister effectively. James wrote: "Don't you realize that friendship with the world makes you an enemy of God? If you want to be a friend of the world, you make yourself an enemy of God. (James 4:4, NLT). It seems strange, but to minister to the world we must be willing to give up our relationship to it. I'm not speaking of the people in the world. We are to love them endlessly. I am speaking of the values and the lifestyle of the world. We must love the people of the world without being in love with the ways of the world! If you don't die to the values and lifestyles of this world, you will lose focus. You will not even think of ministering to others anymore. You will forget why you are here. You will not be a fruit bearing believer.

I was a child when Cassius Clay, or Muhammad Ali, was at his peak. I never watched boxing before, and haven't watched much since; the buzz about this man seemed to have captured the attention of my young boy's imagination. The fights didn't happen very often, and when they did, they were sometimes later in the evening. Occasionally mom and dad would allow my brother and I to stay up past our bed time and watch it, depending on the activities of the next day. Other times we had to go to bed. The nature of our house, however, was that we could sneak out of our bedroom, up the short hall, and peak around the corner. We could look through the dining room, into the living room and get a pretty clear view of the old black and white television, which was sucking signals out of the air with its large antennae reaching out from its space ship like apparatus resting on top. Surely such a scheme must have been my brother's idea. It was amazing to watch the grace and skill of Cassius Clay. In his own words, he "moved like a butterfly, and stung like a bee". Occasionally, however, I would notice that right in the middle of the fight the opponent would stop and hug him. Was it that he secretly had a deep love and appreciation for the skill of his fellow boxer? Despite all of the hype, threats, and predictions of impending doom that Muhammad Ali uttered prior to the match; did he really like this, Ali? The answer is an unequivocal "no". The hugging was not an expression of love. It was a tactic. When Ali got close enough to seriously injure his opponent, the other boxer would wrap his arms around him. Of course, the referee would soon separate them, but in the meantime the hug seriously reduced the impact of any blows to the body. Listen carefully! When we get too close to the world, when we embrace its values and lifestyle, we seriously reduce or nullify our ability to impact it. We cannot bring Christ to the world when we are more in the world than we are in Christ. There must be enough distance between the way we live and the way the world lives for them to see the benefits of our Christianity. There must be enough distance between our value system and theirs for them to see that Christ's way is the better way. If we embrace the world, we can't minister to it. If we die to its values and lifestyle, we can bear godly fruit. "Don't copy the behavior and customs of this world, but let God transform you into a new person by changing the way you think. Then you will learn to know God's will for you, which is good and pleasing and perfect." (Romans 12:2, NLT).

Finally, Samson gave himself completely to Delilah. He told her the secret of his strength. Here is a news flash for you! Samson's strength was not in his hair. Samson's strength was in what the hair symbolized. His hair represented a vow that separated him, or consecrated him to God and His purposes. He made a conscious decision for the things of this world over the ways of God. When Samson spilled the beans to Delilah, it signified that his dedication to God and God's will for his life was over. He made a decision to not do as God had directed. Samson's anointing was gone and he didn't even know it. So, when Delilah warned Samson that the Philistines had come to capture him, he assumed that he would set himself free as he had done previously. Not this time. Rather than dying to self, as the Nazirite vow required, he died to the purposes of God. The supernatural life that flowed through him to give him his amazing strength was no longer there. Flirting with the enemy caused him to fall in love with the enemy. He couldn't fulfil God's purposes now! He no longer had the ability to do what he was placed on this earth to do. Spiritual life flows through the Christian to bear spiritual fruit. When we die to self and live to that end, we have spiritual vitality that gives us the ability to accomplish great things for God's glory. But when we die to the purposes of God we wither spiritually.

"For if you live according to the sinful nature, you will die; but if by the Spirit you put to death the misdeeds of the body, you will live." (Romans 8:13, NIV)

The Philistines used Samson like an animal. He wasn't pretty anymore. They gouged out his eyes. They bound him in bronze shackles, and used him like they would use an ox to grind at the grist mill. When the people saw him, they shouted in celebration that Samson had been delivered to them, giving credit to their false god. It was bad enough that Samson wasn't glorifying God with his life, but a lifeless idol was getting glory for Samson's failure.

Sometime later the Philistines gathered in the temple to offer sacrifices to their god, Dagon. They were becoming artificially happy through alcohol when someone had this great idea to bring Samson into the temple to amuse them. Now the temple was packed with people. All of the Philistine rulers were there. The floor was packed and there were 3,000 people on the roof of the building. They brought Samson in and stood him between the pillars that supported the roof. Then Samson whispered a little prayer that opened the floodgates of God's anointing. He prayed: "Sovereign LORD, remember me again. O God, please strengthen me just one more time. With one blow let me pay back the Philistines for the loss of my two eyes." (Judges 16:28, NLT). He reached out, placing one hand on each pillar. With all his might he began to push. Then he felt that old feeling coming over him again. He knew what this victory would cost him, but he was ready to give himself completely for the purposes of God that day. Finally, Samson was dying to self, temptation, and temporal values. He concluded his prayer by making a vow to God that was even greater than the Nazirite vow. It was a vow to make the ultimate sacrifice to fulfil what he was put on this earth for. Samson said: "Let me die with the Philistines." He no longer pushed with his own physical strength. God's supernatural strength filled him once again, and he began to push. I can only imagine what the drunken crowd on the roof thought when they began to feel the roof shake beneath their feet. I can imagine the band ceasing to play, and the people stopping their dancing as plaster cracks appeared in the walls and the ceiling above them. Perhaps bits of the ceiling began to pelt their heads and upper bodies. Finally, the pillars broke loose. The 3,000 people above fell to their death as the roof caved. The Philistine rulers and the huge crowd of people inside the temple were crushed. Samson died. Scripture records that Samson killed more Philistines in his death than he did during his life. That's the point! When we die we bear fruit. Living for God requires dying to self. That's how we become effective for Him. That's how we become bountiful fruit-bearers.

There are people reading this book that have been Christians for a long time. Many of you are steeped in God's Word. But when you look at the amount of godly fruit you have born you find yourself wanting. Is it possible that you have flirted with the world, and there is little difference between the way you live and the way those around you live? Is it possible that you have been consistently tempted in an area of your life and stopped resisting at some point? Is it possible that the things of this world have taken an undue place on your priority list and have superseded God's priorities for your life? These are not accusations: not at all. They are honest questions we all must ask ourselves from time to time.

You must die to selfish desires. You must die to temptation. You must die to the values and lifestyle of the world, all so that the life of God will flow through you to fulfil His purposes. We bare more godly fruit when we die to self and let the nature of Christ live through us than when we try to live for Him in our own strength. That is the way of fruit-bearing in God's kingdom. The beginning of a fruit bearing plant is always a seed that dies. Immediately following the list of the fruit of the Holy Spirit in Galatians 5, the Apostle Paul wrote: "Those who belong to Christ Jesus have nailed the passions and desires of their sinful nature to his cross and crucified them there. Since we are living by the Spirit, let us follow the Spirit's leading in every part of our lives." (Galatians 5:24-25, NLT)

Part of being united with Christ is to be united with Him in death as well as new life. When we unite with Him in His death, sin loses its effectiveness or power over our lives. Christ destroyed the power of sin through His death at Calvary. So, uniting with Him in death means the death of the old, sinful nature. "He himself bore our sins in his body on the tree, so that we might die to sins and live for righteousness; by his wounds you have been healed." (1 Peter 2:24, NIV). When we unite with Him in new life, the life of Christ by the Holy Spirit is lived through us. Water baptism is a perfect picture or dramatization of this. It is a testimony that the sinful nature was crucified with Christ and we were given new life through Him. That's what Paul was talking about when he wrote: "Since we have been united with him in his death, we will also be raised to life as he was. We know that our old sinful selves were crucified with Christ so that sin might lose its power in our lives. We are no longer slaves to sin. For when we died with Christ, we were set free from the power of sin. And since we died with Christ, we know we will also live with him. We are sure of this because Christ was raised from the dead, and he will never die again. Death no longer has any power over him. When he died, he died once to break the power of sin. But now that he lives, he lives for the glory of God. So you also should consider yourselves to be dead to the power of sin and alive to God through Christ Jesus." (Romans 6:5-11, NLT).

Sin is always a sign that the old nature is still alive and kicking. When Peter denied Jesus those three times after Jesus was arrested, his old nature was fighting for its life. It was fighting for survival. That struggle manifested itself through lies and denying any association with Christ. On the Day of Pentecost, we saw a whole different Peter, who cared nothing about himself. Instead, in the face of great danger, he allowed the life and power of Christ to flow through him with incredible power and remarkable effectiveness. The old nature had been crucified with Christ.

There was no struggle for Elisha. Elisha, in the Old Testament, was called to be a servant to the prophet Elijah. Of course, we would come to know Elisha as a great prophet as well. He was a very well-to-do farmer when he was called to this less than glamorous role. Elijah, under God's direction, approached him. Elisha was ploughing in the field when the prophet came close and simply laid his cloak over Elisha's shoulders, saying nothing, and then riding away. Elisha knew exactly what this meant. His response was priceless. "So Elisha returned to his oxen and slaughtered them. He used the wood from the plow to build a fire to roast their flesh. He passed around the meat to the townspeople, and they all ate. Then he went with Elijah as his assistant." (1 Kings 19:21, NLT). He immediately destroyed the things that represented his current life and selfish desires. He destroyed the things that would make retreat to his old life and values possible. He destroyed the things that represented his significant wealth, a potential distraction away from the will of God. Elisha was a perfect example of how to die to self. Unlike Samson and Peter, death of the old life did not come hard for this man. He was willing to give everything up to serve God by serving Elijah. We know now that the fruit of his life was remarkable.

The life of Christ simply cannot flow through the man or woman whose sinful nature is still alive and kicking. You must die to selfish desires. You must die to temptation. You must die to the values and lifestyle of the world, all so that the life of God will flow through you to fulfil His purposes and bear much godly fruit to the glory of God.

The truth is that people will not be drawn to Christ by seeing us. Quite frankly, without Christ you are not that attractive. At least you are not attractive enough to invoke change in an individual and to cause them to want to give their lives over to God. That will only happen when you die to self and allow the nature of Christ to be seen in you by bearing the fruit of the Holy Spirit. His nature is the fruit that bears fruit. The very next verse, after the list of the fruit of the Holy Spirit, says this: "Those who belong to Christ Jesus have nailed the passions and desires of their sinful nature to his cross and crucified them there." (Galatians 5:24, NLT). In another letter Paul says it all: "He died for everyone so that those who receive his new life will no longer live for themselves. Instead, they will live for Christ, who died and was raised for them." (2 Corinthians 5:15, NLT).

7 MANY TO THE POWER OF ONE

Songs, sermons, articles and books have been written about the necessity of unity within the body of Christ. It is doubtful that, if asked, even one person in any given church would argue its importance. Yet there are few churches not hampered by its lack in one way or another. To impact our geographic community, the church community must be an example of what a united community can accomplish. It is vital to understand that the principles of fruit bearing that apply to us as individuals also apply to the church as a whole. The reason is that the church is intended to be a collection of individuals that operate as one body. In the mind of God, the collective church is the body of Christ - singular. Because of differing personalities, different levels of spiritual maturity, and different ideas of what this body should look like; this is not easily accomplished. It can only be done by every individual purposefully dying to self, bearing the fruit of righteousness, and the fruit of the Holy Spirit.

The community outside of the church is looking for something better. They are not interested in a microorganism that reflects the same problems they experience in the world at large, that they see in the political world, or that they experience in their extended families or their work place. They will not be attracted to something that is the same as what they are already experiencing. They are looking for something better.

They are looking for something ideal, or that is in obvious pursuit of it. They are looking for the kind of community that would be the outcome of each individual within it living the Christ-like life.

Disunity is rampant today. I've seen it. It is destroying the effectiveness of the church throughout the globe. The simplest issue can cause strife within a church and distract it from its purpose. The colour of the new carpet, the way the pastor dresses, the pastor's wife's makeup are all silly issues that have dominated the discussion in the foyer rather than how to grow deeper in our walk with God and how to bear godly fruit for His kingdom. A common phrase that developed in the 1990's is the term "worship war". How can there be division over worship? That term is an oxymoron. Worship cannot cause division. True corporate worship involves everyone getting their eyes off of self and on to the nature of God. The issue has nothing to do with worship. The issue is that people haven't got their eyes off of self at all. It has everything to do with personal preference and people wanting their own 'style' of music. Getting our eyes off of God and on to selfish desires is the root cause of disunity in of any form within the body of Christ. This problem exposes itself through many various issues that have divided churches and rendered them impotent. This was not at all what we saw in the early church where the fruit of righteousness, the fruit of the Holy Spirit, and the fruit of salvations were bountiful.

Because the topic at hand is unity; not disunity, I will be careful to not dwell on the negative for too long. However, it is vital that we are aware of the diseases and parasites that will suck the life out of the church and hamper or destroy its ability to bear fruit. It may not be a complete list, but I perceive four essential root causes. They are 1) the need to control, 2) the need to get one's own way (selfishness), and 3) unresolved differences which can lead to gossip. A brief discussion on each of these is essential. I would love to psycho-analyze these behaviours and determine their root cause, but I am not a psychologist. Anything written would be mere conjecture and personal opinion. What I do know is that there are Scriptural directives that would quickly eradicate the problems if they were followed.

Control

Most churches seem to struggle with at least one person who loves position. They have, what they believe to be, the spiritual gift of 'control'. For whatever reason, they have a need to have things done their way and at their time. Unfortunately, no matter how smooth they try to be, they will eventually hurt others along the way in their quest for influence. They seek after position and prestige within the congregation to legitimize their own need for a place of authority and power. Often, they are easily hurt and over react when they don't get the position they desire or when the church doesn't do things as they think they should be done.

There are Biblical positions of authority in the church to which we must submit. In Acts 6 the twelve Apostles were finding that their time was taken up by too much activity, and not enough time was available to fulfil their role as apostles. Their place was to devote their time to prayer and ministry of the Word of God. They needed someone to administrate the care of the widows. As a result, seven men were chosen. They were men like Stephen, who was full of faith and the Holy Spirit. This leadership model worked, and the Bible records that "God's message continued to spread. The number of believers greatly increased in Jerusalem, and many of the Jewish priests were converted, too." (Acts 6:7, NLT).

As the church grew, God saw fit to appoint certain leadership roles within the church. He would provide the right people with the right spiritual gifts to fulfil those roles. "Now these are the gifts Christ gave to the church: the apostles, the prophets, the evangelists, and the pastors and teachers. Their responsibility is to equip God's people to do his work and build up the church, the body of Christ. This will continue until we all come to such unity in our faith and knowledge of God's Son that we will be mature in the Lord, measuring up to the full and complete standard of Christ." (Ephesians 4:11-13, NLT). The end result of the church following the Biblical leadership model is maturity and unity. God's way is always most effective.

The characteristics of people with leadership positions in the church are laid out for us in I Timothy chapter 3 and in Titus chapter 1. When people with the appropriate Biblical gifting and the characteristics outlined in Scripture are in appropriate leadership positions, the rest of the body is instructed to submit. "Obey your spiritual leaders, and do what they say. Their work is to watch over your souls, and they are accountable to God. Give them reason to do this with joy and not with sorrow. That would certainly not be for your benefit." (Hebrews 13:17, NLT). Spiritual leaders are exactly that. They are spiritual, and they are leaders. They accept their accountability to God with sincerity and awe. They seek to protect the souls of those under their influence. People seeking control, however, are motivated by self-gratification and self-aggrandizement. True motives are always revealed in time. Sincere spiritual leaders will build up the church and lead its members to maturity as they watch carefully over the souls of the church family, while those who seek control will cause division and hurt in an attempt to gain inappropriate influence. This is common in nearly every forum outside the church. It is inexcusable within.

Selfishness

I wish there were a tally of the number of people who have left churches because they weren't being fed, their needs weren't being met, or the pastor didn't do enough for them. It would be astounding. The Biblical reality is that your responsibility within the body of Christ is to minister. It is not to seek a place where you receive the most attention or the best preaching.

Church is a place where others come first. It is a place where you make decisions based on what is best for others in the body. "Don't be concerned for your own good but for the good of others." (1 Corinthians 10:24, NLT). The same writer who penned the previous phrase, the apostle Paul, also wrote this: "Don't be selfish; don't try to impress others. Be humble, thinking of others as better than yourselves." (Philippians 2:3, NLT). Church is about the opportunities you have to give, more than it is about what you receive. If everyone in the church body came with this attitude, not one church member would ever feel like their needs aren't being ministered to. We would all enter the church doors with sensitivity to one another and to the Holy Spirit, seeking an opportunity to minister to someone. In that we would find our fulfilment and satisfaction. At the same time, others within the body would minister to our needs as well. Church would become a place where everyone is watching out for the needs of others. When you touch the lives of others in some positive way you will feel fulfilled in your church. The writer to the Hebrews wrote: "And let us not neglect our meeting together, as some people do, but encourage one another, especially now that the day of his return is drawing near." (Hebrews 10:25, NLT). Do you see why it is necessary to meet together? It is because, in that place of meeting, there will be an opportunity for you to encourage someone.

This is an atmosphere to which those with needs of every kind will be attracted. They will come with a certainty that they will be ministered to. As they mature, they will use the lessons of their past experiences to minister to the needs of others. Church, then, becomes an atmosphere where fruit bears fruit.

Unresolved Differences and Gossip

Gossip is a tool used by Satan to rip apart families, friendships, and churches. This is a temptation that must be resisted. We've all heard this from a parent or mentor: "If you can't say something nice about a person, don't say anything at all." This is a practice that must be followed in church life. Like any form of communication, it takes two people to gossip – one to talk and one to listen. You must refuse to do either. Solomon identified why this is so important: "A troublemaker plants seeds of strife; gossip separates the best of friends." (Proverbs 16:28, NLT). Gossip is a cancer that sucks the life out of any relationship, including the relationship between brothers and sisters in Christ. Not only does it stop our ability to bear fruit, but it is also counterproductive. It hurts and destroys otherwise healthy members in the body of Christ.

Gossip is often caused by unresolved differences between two individuals.

If someone within the fellowship of believers has wronged you in some way, which is often the initiating cause of gossip, the Scripture is very clear about how to handle this. Talking to someone else about the individual will only serve to exasperate or even perpetuate the problem, but solve nothing. This is Jesus' instruction on how to handle our differences: "If another believer sins against you, go privately and point out the offense. If the other person listens and confesses it, you have won that person back. But if you are unsuccessful, take one or two others with you and go back again, so that everything you say may be confirmed by two or three witnesses. If the person still refuses to listen, take your case to the church. Then if he or she won't accept the church's decision, treat that person as a pagan or a corrupt tax collector." (Matthew 18:15-17, NLT). Sometimes people excuse their gossip by saying that they are seeking the opinions and advice of others on how to deal with a situation. Hear this: There is no counsel wiser than that which Jesus gives.

This is so significant that even your worship is meaningless if you have not made wrongs right with fellow believers. In God's eyes the gossiper is no better than the person that has committed the initial offense. One sin is as bad as the other. Gossip could be the initial offense, or it could be the result of not dealing with offenses Biblically. It is still wrong. It is still offensive and sinful. The following are harsh words. Jesus taught: "But I say, if you are even angry with someone, you are subject to judgment! If you call someone an idiot, you are in danger of being brought before the court. And if you curse someone, you are in danger of the fires of hell. So if you are presenting a sacrifice at the altar in the Temple and you suddenly remember that someone has something against you, leave your sacrifice there at the altar. Go and be reconciled to that person. Then come and offer your sacrifice to God." (Matthew 5:22-24, NLT). This includes our worship; our sacrifice of praise.

The fellowship of believers is no place for anger and bad feelings toward one another. As people bearing the fruit of the Holy Spirit, there is no excuse for not being able to work out our differences. If we choose to not do so, we have chosen to not bear the fruit of Christ's nature and have prevented the body of Christ from being able to bear fruit for the kingdom of God. That's not the kind of thing I want to answer for on the Day of Judgment.

Unity Understood

Sometimes it is assumed that if there is no bickering, the church is unified. That is not true. Unity is more than the absence of conflict. Unity is the body of Christ going the same direction, at the same time, for the same purpose. Where unity exists, everything is in alignment. The church's vision is the same. The goals are the same. Everyone is working toward the same end. In this atmosphere the Spirit of God can flow through us corporately, without obstruction, to fulfil His purposes.

On the other hand, the very context of Psalm 133 (to be discussed in more detail later) makes clear that unity does not require uniformity. The Jews that came to Jerusalem to worship at the various feasts and festivals were from many locations. As with today, not all Jewish people lived in Israel. Some were rich while others were poor. Some liked tall, skinny Rabbis while others liked short, heavy-set ones. Some liked young ones that acted mature for their age, while others liked older experienced ones that acted young. Some wanted to sing the psalms to a rock beat, while others preferred southern gospel style. You get the idea. The fact is, when they came together to worship, personal preference didn't matter. All they cared about for the moment was expressing their love to God. That was it! They were there to love God! Nothing else mattered.

This is very important! Our different experiences, preferences, strengths, and weaknesses brought together in unity of focus and purpose is a great strength. God will use our different personalities to increase our fruit bearing capacity as a church when we collectively align them with His will. If we bring our different personalities, strengths and weaknesses to the mount of worship hand in hand, saturated in the Holy Spirit, it will be an amazing atmosphere with amazing potential. Problems only come when the need to be in control, selfish desires, and personal differences get in the way.

Unity is something that we talk about a great deal, and do very little to make happen. It is high on our needs list, but low on our to-do list. We all know how important it is, and yet seem to do more to prevent it than to cause it. The human nature so often prevails when it comes to issues of unity. We drag into church life the very things that fragment other relationships. The same attitudes and behaviours that fragment families, social groups, and other communities sneak in the front door of the church. They often hide behind bibles, suits, pretty dresses, and fancy haircuts. The church must be a uniquely unified body within society as a whole in order to reveal the true nature of the body of Christ. This is what will attract people. This is what will bear fruit. Destructive and divisive behaviours must be kept outside the church walls. That is not to say that ungodly behaviour is appropriate in any context, but the church must stand out as an example of what a community should truly look like. The character of God should run rampant within the church.

Most churches are full of very wonderful people, and they are working hard doing good church things, but I dare say that something is missing. When the church today is compared to the church in Acts 2 through 10 there is very little that can be compared. I would suggest that the ingredient missing most often is unity of spirit, mind, and direction.

When the body is in complete harmony, it invites God's glory and creates an atmosphere through which Christ's anointing can be released. It is really interesting to note that both Romans 12 and 1 Corinthians 12 speaks of gifts of the Holy Spirit, and both of these passages are couched in the context of church unity. Unity is the atmosphere in which the Spirit of God moves freely. It is the place where the anointing is released. It is the place to which the glory of God comes.

Having a church full of wonderful people is not enough to make it a fruit bearing church. Having all the right people with all of the right gifts to make your church a complete body, is not enough to make it a fruit bearing church. If there is not an atmosphere of unity in which the anointing can be released the church will be rendered ineffective. It becomes like the Tin Man in the Wizard of Oz. All the parts are there, but he can't do anything until oil is applied. When all the parts are present in the body of Christ, and the church is in unity, an atmosphere is created where God will pour out His anointing oil. Then the body can operate as it should. Then the gifts of the Holy Spirit as found in Romans 12 and I Corinthians 12 will operate perfectly. Then godly fruit will be born.

The Good Stuff about Unity

The newborn church was a great example of church unity. Prior to her birth the cells that formed the church's fetus were the followers of Jesus. The womb was the upper room. Scripture records that "They all met together and were constantly united in prayer" (Acts 1:14, NLT). The word translated "met together" literally means "with one mind". This same word shows up again in Acts 2:1 "On the day of Pentecost all the believers were meeting together in one place." (Acts 2:1, NLT). They were in one mind in one place. After just ten days of this 'like-mindedness' the Spirit of God fell in remarkable fashion. A sound came that was like a mighty, rushing wind. Tongues of fire rested on each of the followers of Jesus. The same Peter that denied Christ fifty-three days previously now stood and preached to the crowd of people, many of which had once shouted to have Jesus Crucified. Three thousand people came into a personal relationship with Jesus that day. People were amazed and perplexed at the Holy Spirit's work. The church met, with one mind, daily. The book of Acts tells us that the people in the baby church devoted themselves to teaching of the apostles, to fellowship with each other, to breaking of bread, and to praying. They voluntarily shared their possessions, making sure that the less fortunate at least had the necessities of life. The church took on the responsibility of caring for the widows who had no one else to take care of them. Amazing things happened. Here are three of them: "A deep sense of awe came over them all, and the apostles performed many miraculous signs and wonders." (Acts 2:43, NLT). "And each day the Lord added to their fellowship those who were being saved." (Acts 2:47, NLT) The baby church was a perfect example of unity; the impact was phenomenal. God used Peter and John to heal the crippled beggar outside the temple gate. On at least one occasion the place where they met for prayer literally shook with the intensity of God's presence. Within a few days the church grew from 120 to 5,000 people.

A key was that they devoted themselves to the essentials. They devoted themselves to the one they believed in – Jesus. They devoted themselves to a doctrine they believed in – the teachings of Jesus. They devoted themselves to the people they believed in – the fellow followers of Jesus. They lovingly gave all of themselves to those things that fostered spiritual maturity, a sense of community among the believers, and an atmosphere in which godly fruit could be plentiful.

It was of great significance that they were with 'one mind' in this devotion to Jesus and His teachings. "All the believers were united in heart and mind. And they felt that what they owned was not their own, so they shared everything they had. The apostles testified powerfully to the resurrection of the Lord Jesus, and God's great blessing was upon them all." (Acts 4:32-33, NLT). What was at the core of this unity of thought and devotion? We find the answer in Paul's encouragement to the Philippian church. "Is there any encouragement from belonging to Christ? Any comfort from his love? Any fellowship together in the Spirit? Are your hearts tender and compassionate? Then make me truly happy by agreeing wholeheartedly with each other, loving one another, and working together with one mind and purpose. Don't be selfish; don't try to impress others. Be humble, thinking of others as better than yourselves. Don't look out only for your own interests, but take an interest in others, too. You must have the same attitude that Christ Jesus had." (Philippians 2:1-5, NLT). This passage defines church as God intended it to be. Acts chapters 2 through 10 define the results.

Unfortunately, it didn't take long for the human spirit to wreck the godly atmosphere in the early church. The apostle Paul dealt with groups who felt that Gentiles should act like Jews. He had to confront people who preferred one teacher or preacher over another, and point them to Christ. He had to bring correction to a church that was proud of how gracious it was by allowing sin to exist, and he fought against those who felt that greater knowledge translated into spiritual superiority. So, the book of Acts proves that unity is attainable but reveals that it is a constant struggle to maintain.

While the signs of Christ's return are multiplying at warp speed, the church is bickering over inconsequential things. While our neighbours are destined for hell, the church is so occupied with internal issues that we nearly forget that that there is a community in dire need of Christ's love. In, what I believe to be the most critical period in recent history, the church must be careful to not go into 'self-destruct' mode. We must achieve and maintain unity. If the church is a kingdom divided against itself, we don't need Satan to stop our effectiveness. We are doing it ourselves. Only when we obey Christ's law of love and function in unity will we have something to offer the world.

Support from the Psalms

Psalm 133 is well known as the unity chapter in the Bible. Its message is powerful. David wrote it. It is a psalm known as a psalm of ascents. It would be sung at the annual feasts in Israel as the people of Israel from every tribe, every walk of life, and every region would be assembling together to worship God. As they ascended the steps of the temple mount, they would collectively sing songs such as this.

How wonderful and pleasant it is
when brothers live together in harmony!
For harmony is as precious as the anointing oil
that was poured over Aaron's head,
that ran down his beard
and onto the border of his robe.
Harmony is as refreshing as the dew from Mount Hermon that falls on the mountains of Zion.
And there the LORD has pronounced his blessing,
even life everlasting. (Psalms 133:1-3, NLT)

Their different backgrounds, preferences, likes and dislikes were of no consequence. They were coming to worship God! Their focus was on what they had most in common, and that was their love for their creator and Lord. This is what church should be like!

So, for a time of unity, David wrote a song about unity. In his song he teaches us that unity prepares us for the presence of God. It prepares us for being in a place where the Holy Spirit will be poured out all over us.

To help understand a portion of this Psalm, please recall that Peter explains that as New Testament Christians we are viewed by God as a priesthood of believers. To the church, he writes: "you are a chosen people. You are royal priests, a holy nation, God's very own possession. As a result, you can show others the goodness of God, for he called you out of the darkness into his wonderful light." (1 Peter 2:9, NLT). Therefore, when we act as a priesthood, all looking to God in unity, He will reveal Himself to us and pour out His Holy Spirit upon us. "For harmony is as precious as the anointing oil that was poured over Aaron's head, that ran down his beard and onto the border of his robe." Unity provides a venue in which God can pour out His Spirit. Leading up to the Day of Pentecost the church met together daily to pray. They were like a priesthood seeking the anointing. They were with one mind, unified in purpose and in attitude, seeking the promise Christ gave of the coming Holy Spirit. In that atmosphere God poured out His power.

Unity is essential for the anointing of God to be released through the church. Where unity doesn't exist, pride, selfishness, unforgiveness, and lack of submission does. Where those things flourish the Holy Spirit doesn't. If unity doesn't exist, how can we call ourselves a royal priesthood or a holy nation? Unity is a Biblical directive. Without it we are a community in disobedience. Where unity flourishes, however, God can move powerfully in our lives and enable us to bear much fruit to His glory and for the expansion of His kingdom.

The book of Acts not only reveals the power of the Holy Spirit, but His ability to work through a unified church. The Holy Spirit hasn't changed since those early chapters in Acts. He is just as powerful as He ever was. He is just as capable of doing the miraculous and saving the multitudes as He was back then. If you agree that God hasn't changed you must admit that the church that has. It is time, once again, for the church to begin moving the same direction, at the same time, for the same purpose so that the Holy Spirit can move through us in power to bear much fruit.

From scarcely above sea level, Mount Hermon reaches nearly ten thousand feet into the air. It is snowcapped much of the year. The tropical sun vaporizes the water from the swamp lands in the upper Jordan valley. When the mist reaches the snowy slopes of Mount Hermon it immediately condenses, causing heavy dew to fall nightly around its base. Everything is saturated. The land is lush there. It creates beautiful gardens and orchards. It is a fruitful land. That is what David was talking about. "Harmony is as refreshing as the dew from Mount Hermon that falls on the mountains of Zion. And there the LORD has pronounced his blessing, even life everlasting." (Psalms 133:3, NLT) When the world is in turmoil' when the worst drought comes when the world is drying up spiritually; when many churches are literally dying of old age; the church where brothers and sisters dwell together in unity will flourish. This church will be a bountiful orchard bearing godly, eternal fruit for His glory

8 LINES IN THE SAND

Limits are common in most aspects of our lives. Sometimes they are legislated and sometimes not. For example, we are only allowed to go a certain speed in our cars. If we go faster than the speed limit, we are in danger of getting a ticket. I could list a thousand rules that establish lines that aren't to be crossed, but there are many lines that we draw for ourselves. Depending on our taste, we will eat certain foods and not others. For those that don't like heights there is a rung on the ladder that is one step higher than an invisible line. At that point the person is just too high. When making a significant purchase, there is an amount that is acceptable and an amount slightly higher that is too much. There are invisible lines that we draw. There are lines in the sand, if you will, that defines a cutting off point. There are lines we choose not to cross.

People draw these lines when it comes to their relationship with God as well. They draw lines in regard to their expression of worship. To some, standing rigid and mouthing out the words of a three hundred year old hymn is as far as they will go. Others will dance, jump up and down, and wave banners as expressions of their love for God. They have different lines. Some of the most effective Christian workers have theological issues with the baptism of the Holy Spirit, as described in Acts chapter 2, being an experience that is applicable today.

Others move freely in this experience and speak in tongues regularly as the apostle Paul claimed to do in I Corinthians 14:18. They have different lines. These issues serve to make a point, but I really want to discuss our service to God.

God expects complete abandonment of self when it comes to serving Him. Every line we draw that effects our service to Him seriously inhibits our ability to bear fruit. There must be nothing that we are not willing to do for Him. There can be no lines in the sand. To be effective, fruit bearing Christians, we must be willing to abandon ourselves to the nature of the Holy Spirit, the will of God, the anointing of Christ, and the work He leads us to do. This implies the spiritual death of our own nature, our own will, and all attempts to serve Him in our own abilities.

Jesus without Borders

Jesus ministered without limitations. He healed the sick and diseased. He cast out demons. He sailed into wind storms. He blessed the needy. He taught those that wanted to learn. He confronted the religious. If the Spirit led Him into a situation He was willing to go. It meant loving the unlovely, facing persecution, and even putting his life on the line. He completely abandoned Himself to the will of the Father. As with all things, He is the perfect example of how we must serve God.

There was one occasion where Jesus literally drew a line in the sand. Its purpose was different however. He did it to reveal the limitations that others placed on their ability to love and forgive, and to reveal that those limitations did not exist in Him. While Jesus was teaching in the Temple courts, the Pharisees brought a woman caught in the act of adultery. The Old Testament law taught that such a woman should be stoned to death. It was a test for Jesus that they were sure that He would fail. Jesus said nothing, but bent down to write in the dirt with His finger. "They kept demanding an answer, so he stood up again and said, "All right, but let the one who has never sinned throw the first stone!" (John 8:7, NLT). One by one the onlookers left, until only Jesus and the woman remained. He looked in her shameful eyes and said: "'Where are your accusers? Didn't even one of them condemn you?' 'No, Lord,' she said. And Jesus said, 'Neither do I. Go and sin no more.'" (John 8:10-11, NLT). When it came to loving and forgiving others, the line that the Pharisees drew was shorter than the one they had drawn for themselves. They could easily excuse their own sin but were quick to point out the sins of others. Jesus put a spot light on a double standard in the Pharisees, and at the same time showed that His ability to love and forgive was without limitations.

Tax collectors were employees of the Roman government that often abused their position of authority to extract more money than required from individuals to gain personal wealth. Typically, the Jews hated them. Matthew, the disciple of Jesus, was a tax collector. Jesus saw past Matthew's sin and saw the potential within him. While most would have nothing to do with him, Jesus called Matthew to be one of his elite followers. Zacchaeus was a tax collector as well. Although most hated him, Jesus fellowshipped with him. In the end, Zacchaeus used his wealth to make restitution to those he had stolen from and to help the poor. There were no limits on whom Jesus would minister to.

People possessed by demons can behave in many different ways. No matter how the demons manifest themselves through an individual, it always ends up being ugly. It is always unlikeable. These are the type of people that most would choose to avoid. Mary Magdalene, who became close friends with Jesus' mother and Jesus Himself, was one of those people. Early in His ministry Jesus cast seven demons from Mary (Luke 8:2). On another occasion, Jesus crossed the Sea of Galilee, landing in a place called Gadara. There was a man there that was so controlled by demons that he was unclothed and lived in the tombs. The townspeople were horrified of this man. Jesus saw past his ugliness and saw a valuable human being. He delivered him from the legion of demons that controlled him. "People rushed out to see what had happened. A crowd soon gathered around Jesus, and they saw the man who had been freed from the demons. He was sitting at Jesus' feet, fully clothed and perfectly sane, and they were all afraid." (Luke 8:35, NLT). Clearly there were no limits that would restrict who Jesus would minister to.

The woman at the well was not only morally corrupt, she was from Samaria. Jews did not like Samaritans. The piece of land on which they lived and worshipped was between Galilee and Judea. It was normally avoided by most. After all, the Samaritans worshipped in a place other than Jerusalem. In the mind of most Jews that was reason enough to shun them. The Samaritans were viewed by most Jews as many Christians would view members of certain cults today. But Jesus had a divine appointment with a Samaritan woman who had been married five times and was currently in a common-law relationship. Jesus reached out to her. As a result of

His ministry to this one woman, he ministered for two whole days in Samaria, where many chose to follow Him. There was no depth of immorality and no religious history that would place limits on Jesus' willingness to minister.

Jesus reached out to the diseased and the healthy, the outcast and the well-accepted, the rich and the poor. His ministry crossed every line of immorality, religion, and disease. He drew no lines in the sand when it came to His willingness to reach out, love, and forgive. His love even circumvented Old Testament laws. He touched the leprous, forgave the adulterous, and healed on the Sabbath. There were simply no limits to restrict what lives Jesus would touch.

New Testament Lines

The apostle Peter was in the city of Joppa. It was in this same city that Jonah, many hundreds of years before, boarded a ship leaving for Tarshish in an attempt to avoid the call of God on his life. He had drawn a line in the sand and was doing all he could to avoid crossing it. It took a large fish with a big mouth and the loud voice of God to get Jonah to cross that line. Now, Peter is in the same city. He was staying at the house of Simon whose business was tanning leather. It was around the noon hour that Peter went to the roof of the house, where he could feel the gentle breezes and smell the salt air from the Mediterranean Sea while he prayed. He was praying, but clearly not fasting. When his growling stomach drowned out the sound of the crashing waves against the shore, Peter requested for his lunch to be prepared. As he waited, something very strange happened. He fell into a trance. Peter had a crazy vision. "He saw the sky open, and something like a large sheet was let down by its four corners. In the sheet were all sorts of animals, reptiles, and birds. Then a voice said to him, 'Get up, Peter; kill and eat them.' 'No, Lord,' Peter declared. 'I have never eaten anything that our Jewish laws have declared impure and unclean.' But the voice spoke again: 'Do not call something unclean if God has made it clean.' The same vision was repeated three times. Then the sheet was suddenly pulled up to heaven." (Acts 10:11-16, NLT). God was about to erase a line in the sand. Peter was still confused by the vision when three men arrived at Simon's house asking if Peter was present. The apostle was assured by the Holy Spirit that it was okay to go meet these Gentile strangers.

Previous to all of this, God spoke to a leader in the Roman army through a vision of an angel. This Gentile's name was Cornelius. He and his family were God-fearing, praying, and generous people. God loved them. It was this angel that instructed Cornelius to send messengers to look for someone named Simon Peter at Simon the tanner's house in Joppa. Two amazing things happened. First, Peter invited the three Gentiles to spend the night. This was unheard of. Jews would never develop such a close relationship with a Gentile that they would invite them to be overnight guests. Second, Peter willingly travelled with a Roman Soldier and two Gentile household servants to see a Roman Centurion in the city of Caesarea. God was erasing a line in the sand. They arrived the next day where they met with Cornelius. This was Peter's response: "You know it is against our laws for a Jewish man to enter a Gentile home like this or to associate with you. But God has shown me that I should no longer think of anyone as impure or unclean. So, I came without objection as soon as I was sent for. Now tell me why you sent for me." (Acts 10:28-29, NLT). Peter preached about Jesus to Cornelius' family and friends. The Holy Spirit fell on them and they began to speak in tongues just as the Jews did on the day of Pentecost.

What the new Jewish Christians couldn't have understood prior to these miraculous events is that God could love a Gentile. It was not in their religious sites. Their doctrines would not allow their minds to go there. He was their God and theirs alone. In their minds, Jesus was the Jewish Messiah. After these phenomenal events, however, Peter came to this conclusion: "I see very clearly that God shows no favoritism. In every nation he accepts those who fear him and do what is right. This is the message of Good News for the people of Israel—that there is peace with God through Jesus Christ, who is Lord of all." (Acts 10:34-36, NLT). God shows no favouritism! His is Lord of all!

This struggle continued between Jew and Gentile for many years to come. Even those who accepted that Gentiles could be in relationship with God, through faith in Jesus Christ, expected them to live by Jewish rites and rituals. This line in the sand caused division in many Christian communities and significantly impacted the church's ability to bear fruit for the kingdom of God.

Lines on Your Faith

There are two lines connected to our Christianity that many Christians die having never crossed. These lines render Christians ineffective. Once we know the truth of the Gospel of Jesus Christ, and His ability to do His work through us, we must cross the line of faith believing and step into the application of that faith. It is important to understand that faith that God can use us and applying that faith in our daily lives are the two separate lines that must be crossed. There are many Christians who have no doubt about God's greatness and His ability to use people in unbelievable ways. They see God using ordinary people in extraordinary ways all the time. They have crossed the first faith line. They just can't believe that God can use them. When called on, they cannot apply their faith to their specific circumstance. Even though God has done great things in their life, they feel inadequate to testify. Although they know that God desires for all to come to know Him, they feel incapable of being used as an instrument of reconciliation. Although they are certain of God's unlimited ability, they can't lay hands on someone and pray with faith, believing for a miracle right then and there.

If it isn't a "can't" issue, it is a detachment issue. For example, many if not most detach themselves from the command to "Go into all the world and preach the Good News to everyone." (Mark 16:15, NTL). They make it the responsibility of the 'church', the 'evangelist', the 'pastor', or the 'youth leader' when in their minds they know full well that it is a command given to all believers. It is a line they don't want to cross because it is hard to apply faith to themselves in that situation. It is hard for them to believe that God can use them to lead someone to Christ. As a result people find a way to subconsciously detach themselves from the responsibility. The human mind's ability to disconnect itself from the truth allows us to live free of guilt and feelings of irresponsibility while not fulfilling our spiritual obligations.

Recently, I was speaking with a youth leader about why the young people in his group have a difficult time inviting their unbelieving peers to their activities. He made a statement that absolutely verified the truth of this point. He said: "They have not yet connected their faith to the great commission." In other words, they believe in God. They believe in God's ability to use people. What they haven't done is attach their faith to the responsibility that is theirs as Christians.

There are a multitude of wonderful, good living Christian people that are accomplishing very little for the kingdom of God because they can't cross one of these two lines. Even though they know and understand that God is all-powerful, they have a hard time believing for God to work through them in powerful ways. Once they get past that line of faith, they run up against another; and that is the application of that faith. They struggle with knowing how to apply their faith to the specific ministry opportunities God gives them. Their knowledge of the presence of the Holy Spirit in their lives to help them in every situation can't seem to be released into the activity of their daily lives. They struggle believing that God can use them to lead their family and friends to a saving knowledge of Jesus Christ. They struggle believing that God's unlimited power can flow through them when they pray. So, they detach themselves from the responsibility.

Ugly Lines

Let's face it. Most of us are guilty of drawing the line as far as who we will minister to. Many can easily pass by the homeless, the alcoholic, the drug addict, and the purple haired teen displaying colourful tattoos and multiple piercings. There are only two likely reasons for this. You either assume that they are a waste of time; too far gone for Jesus to be able to save them, or your ability to apply Christ's unconditional love has proven to have conditions. Either way, by not reaching out to these people, you are making a decision that could impact the eternal destiny of some of the 'whosoever will' that Christ came to die for.

Another group that are often ignored is the higher class of our society – the wealthy, the doctors, and the lawyers. Again, there are two likely reasons. You make an assumption that these people are well enough off that they would not acknowledge their need for a Saviour. The other likelihood is that you assume that they are so much more intelligent than you that you couldn't possibly minister to them effectively.

Another group that is often ignored, if not despised, is the religious. I'm speaking of the ones who knock on your door on Saturday morning, but you won't answer. I'm talking about the ones who look Christian, but have a totally different view of who Jesus is than what the Word teaches. I'm speaking of those who do Christian things but don't believe in being 'born again'. I'm speaking of those who think that salvation comes through rites and rituals rather than relationship. There are many religious groups that we evangelicals write off as being impossible to reach. They argue too much. They are too deceived. They are too caught up in their religion to hear our message. Whatever the reason, we avoid reaching out to them with the truth of the Gospel.

How quickly we discount the power of the Holy Spirit to touch the complete spectrum of society. We rapidly assume that those on the extremes are unreachable. We assume that the deceived will never see the truth. We have concluded that the Holy Spirit cannot change such lives. I can almost hear the resounding outcry: "That's not true! That's not how I feel at all. The

Holy Spirit can touch and change any life." This is a situation where we know and believe what the Spirit of God is capable of, but our actions prove that we have drawn a line in the sand. When we choose to not minister to someone, we are deeming them unreachable by God through us. Do we really want that responsibility? Do we really view ourselves as worthy of making that kind of judgment?

Whenever we can walk by someone and quietly conclude that there is no point in ministering to them – we have drawn a line. None of us have such a privilege. Jesus command was for us to go into ALL the world. His example to us was to minister to every level of society. He ministered to the downcast, the outcast, the religious, the average, and the exceptional. There were no lines. He came to die for everybody. So must we.

Uncertain Lines

Many Christians, young and old in the faith, feel inadequate to share the gospel to certain people. That is nobody's fault but your own. Peter said: "if someone asks about your Christian hope, always be ready to explain it." (1 Peter 3:15, NLT).

There is an obligation on each of us to know the fundamentals of our faith to a degree that we can answer the questions of those seeking truth. That goes beyond rote answers. We must be certain of what we believe and knowledgeable about our faith. We need to understand the fundamentals of Christianity in a way that we can communicate with assurance, authority, and conviction.

It is amazing the number of Christians whose lives have been changed by the truth of the gospel, and yet their understanding of that truth remains superficial because of a lack of willingness to study and know God's Word. They can easily vegetate in front of the television, video game, or sporting activity for 3 or 4 hours in an evening; yet have little or no time to study God's Word. Even some people who have been Christians for many years often have a very shallow understanding of the Bible. The writer to the Hebrews addressed this issue with his readers: "You have been believers so long now that you ought to be teaching others. Instead, you need someone to teach you again the basic things about God's word. You are like babies who need milk and cannot eat solid food. For someone who lives on milk is still an infant and doesn't know how to do what is right. (Hebrews 5:12-13, NLT).

A Line that is Too Short

Sometimes we do the right thing, but just don't go far enough. For example, Jesus told us to "go and make disciples of all the nations" (Matthew 28:18, NIV), yet we are happy to go downtown and make converts. We are content when someone responds to an altar call in our church. We breathe a big sigh of relief when someone prays the sinner's prayer. We give them a tract or book with the church name on it, and we pat ourselves on the back for doing our job as a Christian. We feel good, and so we should. The angels rejoice with us at that moment. But, please understand that if we are making converts and not disciples, we are not completely fulfilling the great commission.

Being evangelical is a commitment. Fruit bearing requires devotion to a process that does not happen overnight. You don't go to bed on a warm spring evening with the sweet scent of apple blossoms wafting through your bedroom window and wake up in the morning with juicy red apples on the tree. There is a ripening or maturing process. The tree owner needs to take necessary steps to prevent worms and disease from destroying the fruit. The apple is an apple the moment that blossom turns into a little green ball. However, it is not all that it must be until it reaches a point where it can be fruitful itself. In the same sense, as much as a person is completely born again upon sincerely repenting of their sin before God, we have an obligation as Christians and as churches to invest in their lives so that they mature into fruitful Christians themselves. We are to make disciples. That means that we are not just there to lead them to faith in Christ, but to become true representatives of Christ.

The church will do this through programs, Bible studies, and courses. These efforts can be very effective. But, for a new believer, there is nothing like sitting around the kitchen table of the person who first prayed with them when they accepted Christ, reading Scripture, and talking about the wonderful truths of God's Word. To be real fruit bearers we must be committed to the process of discipleship both individually and as a church body.

The "All about Me" Lines

It is interesting to talk to Christians about why they find it difficult to witness or to get involved in certain ministries in the church. The reason most often given is fear. If we were to ask those people what they are afraid of, it sometimes relates to the previous section on uncertainty about their beliefs. Perhaps even more often it is fear of rejection. It is fear of someone not liking them. Perhaps it is fear of doing harm to an existing relationship with a friend, co-worker, or family member that they sincerely desire to come to know Jesus. In this case, what they interpret as being fear looks an awful lot like pride to the discerning onlooker.

I don't want to sound judgmental in this, because no one wants to do harm to a relationship that is important to them. I believe that there are ways to sensitively and consistently reveal the character of Christ that ultimately results in the opportunity to verbally share the truth about the Saviour to our loved ones. Having said that, let me emphasize the importance of eventually, at the appropriate time, getting to the place where we encourage those close to us to accept Christ as their personal Saviour and Lord. Surely, if you truly care about them, you long for them to share the same hope of eternal life that you do.

Returning to the issue at hand, the thing that so often prevents us from sharing our faith is too often pride. It is concern about what others will think of us. We overshadow the importance of their salvation with concerns about how we would feel if they reject us. Whether we speak to them about Jesus, or not, must be out of concern for how they will feel if rejected by God. We must step over the line of our own pride, and risk it for the sake of those who just might spend eternity in hell if we don't explain the way of life.

Lines to Protect the Safe Place

To many people church is their safe place. So it should be. You have special friends there. You can express yourself freely in worship there. You can be open about your love for God there. It's great! It is your Sunday haven from the normal activities of life. The problem is that your normal activities of life don't necessarily reflect your love for God and a heart full of worship. Bringing in people from 'the outside world' will mean that something has to change. To be viewed as something less than a hypocrite, either your life inside or outside the church will need to be adjusted so that they are in line with each other. You will either have to scale down your expression of love for God in church, or make it more a part of your life outside of church. That could mean that either your Christian friends will think you are backsliding or your non-Christian friends will think that you have become a religious fanatic. So, you draw a clear line between those two worlds. The comfortable thing to do is to keep the people in your weekday world outside of the church walls, and those in your Sunday world inside – and never the two shall meet. The problem is that the people in your outside-the-church world really need a Saviour.

The other problem, of course, is that to bring people in the church from the outside could change the dynamics of your particular social network there. To add another personality or personalities could change everything. Sharing your friends at church with someone you are friends with through another connection is something you're just not prepared to do. The risk of making the safe place vulnerable to change is enough to prevent you from inviting others in.

This chapter is a call to honesty with ourselves. It calls attention to the frailty of our logic for not bearing godly fruit. It calls our attention to undeniable limits that we place on our love for the lost, even though we talk and pray as if we do love them without condition. Our actions prove that this love is not great enough to make us cross the lines we have drawn. Jesus talked about picking up our cross daily. If the cross that Jesus spoke of represents a place that we just don't want to go in our service to Him; if it represents a dangerous place to us, an ugly place, and place that is beyond reason, then we need to learn to cross the cross daily. We need to abandon everything for the purpose of bearing godly fruit, and cross the lines we have unwittingly established. Those lines are keeping people from the same kind of relationship with God that we enjoy. They are ultimately keeping people from the hope of eternity. Every one of these lines can be erased with a simple change of attitude and a little effort. Today is the day to get the eraser out.

9 A STERN WARNING

This book has been challenging. That is the intent. Challenge is what makes us grow beyond where we are. It is a good thing. However, compared to Jesus' discussion on this topic, Fruit Loose and Fancy Tree has been a cakewalk.

An excessively large crowd had gathered around Jesus. He taught many things to these curious listeners. This was one of His parables: "Then Jesus told this story: "A man planted a fig tree in his garden and came again and again to see if there was any fruit on it, but he was always disappointed. Finally, he said to his gardener, 'I've waited three years, and there hasn't been a single fig! Cut it down. It's just taking up space in the garden.' "The gardener answered, 'Sir, give it one more chance. Leave it another year, and I'll give it special attention and plenty of fertilizer. If we get figs next year, fine. If not, then you can cut it down.'" (Luke 13:6-9, NLT). We see the grace of God in this story. We see his patience. We see a level of understanding that time may be needed for us to reach a higher stage of spiritual maturity and the resulting productivity. Yet it is clear that there are limits to His willingness to extend His boundless grace to those who choose to remain fruitless believers.

Jesus is more specific in his teaching on this subject at the time that the apostle John records it. "I am the true grapevine, and my Father is the gardener. He cuts off every branch of mine that doesn't produce fruit, and he prunes the branches that do bear fruit so they will produce even more. You have already been pruned and purified by the message I have given you. Remain in me, and I will remain in you. For a branch cannot produce fruit if it is severed from the vine, and you cannot be fruitful unless you remain in me.

"Yes, I am the vine; you are the branches. Those who remain in me, and I in them, will produce much fruit. For apart from me you can do nothing. Anyone who does not remain in me is thrown away like a useless branch and withers. Such branches are gathered into a pile to be burned. But if you remain in me and my words remain in you, you may ask for anything you want, and it will be granted! When you produce much fruit, you are my true disciples. This brings great glory to my Father.

"I have loved you even as the Father has loved me. Remain in my love. When you obey my commandments, you remain in my love, just as I obey my Father's commandments and remain in his love. I have told you these things so that you will be filled with my joy. Yes, your joy will overflow!" (John 15:1-11, NLT).

The True Vine

All spiritual life and vitality flows through and out from Jesus. Without Him we can do good things. We can do good works. We can be good people. But we can't do anything of eternal value. We cannot bear the fruit of the Holy Spirit, we cannot bear the fruit of righteousness in a way that truly reflects the nature of Christ, and we will lose both the desire and the spiritual impetus to lead others to Christ.

It is truly amazing that, knowing this, we give such little attention in our day to day lives to nurturing our relationship with Him. When we are physically hungry, we eat. When we are physically tired, we rest. When we are physically ill, we do what's necessary to gain strength. We fail to recognize, however, that when we are spiritually hungry, tired, or ill; Christ is always what we need. Many acknowledge it verbally, but this truth isn't so engrained in them that it changes their behaviour. We need to find spiritual vitality in Him on a daily basis. We need to learn to feed on Him through the reading of His Word and prayer. Christ Himself, while incarnate, placed more value on the Word for spiritual sustenance than bread for physical sustenance. While being tempted by Satan to turn a stone into bread, during a forty day fast in the desert, Jesus responded: "People do not live by bread alone, but by every word that comes from the mouth of God. " (Matthew 4:4, NLT). Christ is our source of life. He is the very breath of our spiritual existence. After all, He said Himself: "I am the bread of life. Whoever comes to me will never be hungry again. Whoever believes in me will never be thirsty." (John 6:35, NLT). The Bible is the food He provides for our soul. Still, there are many believers who rarely think to pick up their Bibles for the purpose of sustaining spiritual life. In addition to feeding on His Word, when we are spiritually tired, we need to learn to rest in Him through absolute faith and trust. And, when we feel broken or sick in our spirits, causing spiritual drudgery and ineffectiveness, we need to acknowledge that enhancing our relationship with Him is what causes spiritual life and vitality to flow through us.

There is a chorus that we used to sing when I was growing up in church. Upon remembering this, I was struck by the simplicity of both the music and the lyrics of some of the older songs. Still they were meaningful and impactful. This chorus went like this:

He is all I need
He is all I need
Jesus is all I need
He is all I need
He is all I need
Jesus is all I need

You can't get much simpler or much more profound than that. Oh, I've heard philosophical arguments against this chorus, but when it comes to our spiritual life it is absolutely true. Life comes from Christ and Christ alone.

Suckers and Wimps

The passage hasn't been tough at all so far, but now Jesus presents the challenge. Speaking of the Heavenly Father, who is the gardener in the analogy, "He cuts off every branch of mine that doesn't produce fruit" (John 15:2, NLT). It is important to note that these branches belong to Jesus. They are part of the vine. They are tapped into His life source, but they are not being productive. Jesus is speaking of people who are like sucker branches that you see on certain types of plants or trees. They are often very straight branches. They have plenty of leaves on them, but they never bear fruit. All they are doing is taking life out of the plant without fulfilling any real purpose. The prudent gardener knows that to cut those branches away will increase the fruitfulness of the other branches. The Heavenly Father is a prudent gardener.

There are people in the church that boldly claim the promises of God. Their testimony includes a very sincere experience with the living Christ, who came into their heart and gave them new birth. They are quick to claim all the benefits of Christianity. They are the first at the altar to have prayer for some blessing. They openly and boldly express their worship in the church service. Outside the church, however, is a totally different thing. The fruit of the Holy Spirit and their behaviour is completely contradictory to each other. They are not loving. Their hearts are full of turmoil and worry, not peace. Patience is a virtue that is foreign to them, and they are quick to express their anger rather than the gentleness of Christ. The people around them see anything but the character of Jesus in their behaviour. There is nothing about their lives that would draw others to Jesus. Some have no issue with wasting away their money while leaving bills unpaid, ruining any hope of a testimony to their landlord or other creditor. Others involve themselves in lifestyle activities that do not reflect that holiness of their Saviour. Their language and behaviour are reprehensible. These people are sucking the life out of the testimony that Christ should have in their community, making it even more difficult for real fruit bearers to accomplish anything for Christ. Their choice to not bear godly fruit and to suck the life out the testimony of others will result in being cut off from the life of Christ.

Near the end of the analogy, we find a second group of people whose choices cause them to be separated from their spiritual life source - Jesus. Earlier, Jesus said: "For a branch cannot produce fruit if it is severed from the vine, and you cannot be fruitful unless you remain in me." (John 15:4, NLT). In verse 6 He states that: "Anyone who does not remain in me is thrown away like a useless branch and withers. Such branches are gathered into a pile to be burned." (John 15:6, NLT). This group fails to nurture their relationship with Jesus. Whether by conscious decision or by spiritual anorexia, they disconnect themselves from their life-source. We've all seen it on plants and trees, where a windstorm or some other event causes a weaker branch to be partially broken and hang loosely from the branch or trunk that it is attached to. It seems okay for a while, but after some time the leaves begin to slowly change colour and wither. Once that starts it soon becomes obvious that the branch is dying. It is unattractive, in the way, and can sometimes even cause danger if it isn't removed. The astute horticulturalist will remove the branch and set it aside for disposal. Jesus is talking about people like that. Perhaps they were too weak spiritually to withstand the storms of life. Or, perhaps the temptation of the world caused them to turn their back on Christ. Without life flowing through them, they are dying. Neither they, nor others see it happening at first. Eventually it becomes obvious. It is seen clearly in their attitude and their actions that they are withering spiritually. They are no longer able to contribute to the kingdom of God. They are becoming useless. Their immaturity or their poor choices will lead them to being set aside where the withering process will complete itself, and they will be burned. Those are very scary words.

What we can't forget is that, in either case, this is not the desire of God. He is not a cruel gardener hoping to find fruitless and withering branches. He is not a Heavenly Father who prowls around seeking whom He may devour. That is what Satan does. God is gracious and loving. He is patient and understanding. When a person, however, chooses to do damage to the kingdom of God because of a conflict between their testimony and their lifestyle. they have chosen for themselves to be cut off. When a person allows themselves to become spiritually weak and fragile to the point where they can't withstand the storms or temptations of life, they have chosen for themselves to be set aside, awaiting their eternal destiny.

This may be an issue of God's judgment, but even more so, it is an issue of Lordship in the life of Christians. It is not enough to just make God our Saviour. Don't misunderstand me. That is an awesome and potentially life changing event. Our eternal destiny is altered at that moment. We are no longer heading toward hell, but toward heaven. I say that it is "potentially" a life changing event because that only comes when we go one step beyond salvation and make Him Lord of our life. If we don't submit ourselves to Him in every area of our life we will continue to live for self. Those are the people who become sucker branches in the church. They have a good testimony of salvation, but the evidence of change in their life is limited or non-existent. The effect of their good testimony is not only eradicated by the way they live, it does harm to God's kingdom. The other danger is that they remain spiritually weak because they don't regularly tap into their source of life and strength. They are therefore unable to withstand temptation or turmoil. They are quick to lose faith or determination in their walk with God. They are cut off from the spiritual life birthed in them at salvation. They die spiritually and are rendered ineffective.

Understand that it is not God's will for anyone to perish (see Matthew 18:7-14). Jesus died so that it would be possible for the whole world to come to salvation. The reality of that salvation, however, will be evident in the fruit that we bear or lack of it. It's a stern warning.

God and Prunes

It doesn't sound so pleasant, but this statement is a good thing: "he prunes the branches that do bear fruit so they will produce even more." (John 15:2, NLT). There are two ways to apply this challenging statement. It can be applied corporately and it can be applied personally.

There are times when churches seem to suffer losses. Occasionally people leave to go to another church or they stop going to church at all. Sometimes they are honest about the reasons, sometimes not, and sometimes they just quietly become invisible. In either case, someone who was once part of your church family is no longer there, and it hurts. Don't get me wrong; the reasons for people deciding to worship elsewhere may be very valid and legitimate. Very often, however, it is God pruning the church. He is removing people who are drawing from the spiritual life of the church but not bearing any fruit. He is cutting away others who fill a pew every Sunday, but they are no longer connected to the vine. They have little or no spiritual life left in them. When they are removed from the place of fellowship they very quickly wither and die in their spirit. Both of these groups of people have had a negative effect on the ability of the church to bear godly fruit in your community. Like you, God would prefer that these individuals be productive members of your fellowship, but they are continuously making life choices that prevent that from being the case.

God has a purpose for your church. He has a job for your church to do in your community. When individuals make conscious decisions that will hamper or prevent the church's ability to do that, God has no choice but to do some pruning. He has no choice but to do some cutting away. Occasionally there is bleeding involved. In the cutting process, the nature of people's hearts are often revealed. Often it is seen through inappropriate expressions of anger, false accusations, and gossip. Things are said with the intent of causing pain. These things hurt, and the church bleeds for a time, but the Spirit of Christ continues to flow through the church to bring healing and even greater strength. She is now even more able to fulfil the purposes of God and bear much fruit; but the individuals who are cut away are in spiritual danger. The Spirit of Life is no longer flowing through them. They no longer have that spiritual vitality that enables them to heal. Pray for them! The church has experienced short term pain, but they are dying. Pray that they acknowledge the choices that have brought them to this place and that they are grafted back in to the church. If not your church, some church. Otherwise, their spiritual destiny is bleak.

God sees the church as an individual, a body, so He prunes it just like He does the individual members within the body. Pruning can be a very personal thing also. Whole trees are pruned as are individual branches. You are a branch. If you are a fruit bearing branch God will lovingly cut those things away from your life that are reducing the amount, or the quality of the fruit that you are bearing.

There are certainly some Biblical examples that support this. You will remember when Jesus was inquiring of the disciples as to who people were saying that He was, and finally who the disciples believed He was. Peter answered correctly: "You are the Messiah. " (Mark 8:29). Jesus was very pleased with that answer. He went on to predict His own persecution and eventual death, after which Peter took Jesus aside and rebuked Him. Jesus' response was quick: "Get away from me, Satan!" he said. "You are seeing things merely from a human point of view, not from God's." (Mark 8:33, NLT). He was cutting away the restrictions caused by Peter's natural thinking. When we are unwilling to seek the mind of God first we end up relying on our feeble human wisdom, and will be guilty of doing things our own way, in our own strength. When we live this way we are extremely vulnerable. Our thoughts and desires are self-serving at the very least. Even worse, it is very possible that we could align our actions with the will of Satan rather than the will of God. This is what happened with Peter. In Peter's natural mind, and for what seemed to be a right motive, he did not want Christ to suffer or die. Neither did Satan. Peter's and Satan's desire were unwittingly in perfect alignment with each other. That is the danger of living and thinking purely in the natural. For Peter to become the great man of God that he did, Jesus had to cut away that inclination to default to his own will and learn to live by the Spirit.

There is a good example in the Apostle Paul's life as well. Yes, perfect Paul wouldn't have been so perfect if it weren't for a little pruning. He had this thing. The Bible calls it both a thorn in his flesh and a messenger from Satan. Whatever it was, God refused to remove it from him. He left it there on purpose. No matter what you call it, it was God's pruning device. Paul himself records: "to keep me from becoming proud, I was given a thorn in my flesh, a messenger from Satan to torment me and keep me from becoming proud. "Three different times I begged the Lord to take it away. Each time he said, "My grace is all you need. My power works best in weakness." So now I am glad to boast about my weaknesses, so that the power of Christ can work through me." (2 Corinthians 12:7-9, NLT). The "thorn" was there for the express purpose of keeping Paul from pride and to cause Him to walk in dependence on God. This enabled him to bear much fruit for God's eternal Kingdom. God didn't put the thorn there, be He didn't take it away either. It served a valuable purpose in Paul's life. Satan may have intended it for evil, but God used it for good. Pride could very well have kept Paul from being the great man of God that he was. It could have been a stumbling block in his walk with the Lord.

God may use circumstance as pruning devices in our lives too. He may also convict us by His Holy Spirit, just like the words of Jesus convicted Peter. His preferred tool, however, is His Word. "For the word of God is alive and powerful. It is sharper than the sharpest two-edged sword, cutting between soul and spirit, between joint and marrow. It exposes our innermost thoughts and desires." (Hebrews 4:12, NLT). The Word is a sharp tool. Those are the best. Brain surgeons rarely use teaspoons in the operating room. The sharper the tool, the less damage there is when cutting or pruning takes place. It provides a clean cut with the least amount of pain and the quickest healing time. The Bible is a tool that can cut away any thought or motive that will restrict our ability to be prolific fruit bearers.

It was an honour for Peter to hear those challenging words. It meant that Jesus saw him as worthy of pruning. Jesus saw the potential for impetuous Peter to be a great fruit bearer. It was through Peter's preaching that 3,000 people cried out for salvation on the day of Pentecost. Paul carried his thorn in the flesh around as a badge of honour. He boasted about his weakness, because then the power of Christ could work through him. It was in his own weakness and Christ's power that Paul won countless numbers to Jesus, started an untold number of churches, and spread the Gospel throughout the then known world. We have the Word of God. God has given it to us because He knows that if we obey it we can become great fruit bearers. To those of you that have this as the desire of your heart, let the Word of God cut to the very core of your thoughts and motives. Let it cut away the suckers and the lifeless things of your life in order that you might be a great fruit bearing believer.

Hang In There

Christ's letter to the church in Laodicea as recorded in the book of Revelation chapter 3 addresses this issue perfectly. It is a church full of people on the fence. They are neither hot nor cold. They say 'yes' to the things of God, profess to be Christian, but live completely fruitless lives. In fact the contradiction between their testimony and their lifestyle is detrimental to the cause of Christ. They are self-sufficient people who express belief in God, but don't really have a sense of need for God. They find their satisfaction in their material wealth rather than in Him. The church in Laodicea is a literal fulfilment of Paul's prophetic words in 2 Timothy 3:5 that the church would have a form of godliness, but deny its power. Their relationship with God was nothing more than form. It may have been a real relationship at one time, but was now reduced to lifeless and powerless religion.

Christ's response to them was that He would rather they be hot or cold, not lukewarm as they were. Their lukewarm Christianity is obnoxious to Him. It sickens Him. He says that He will soon have to spit them out of His mouth. It seems harsh, but it is completely consistent with our earlier discussion. There is a point at which God says that He can't take any more of our sins of omission – not doing the things He taught us to do. If we want Him as our Saviour we must make Him Lord as well. That means being a fruit bearing believer. God is not anxious to cut people away from the vine or to spit them out of His mouth; but quite frankly there is a job to be done. The Kingdom of God must be extended around the world, and that is the job of the church. We must be true representatives of His holiness, His Character, and effective ministers of His Gospel. Not participating in these instructions is just as much a sin as breaking one of the Ten Commandments. He cannot withstand people who want the best of both worlds: sitting on the fence, having one foot in the world and one in the church, bringing dishonour to the cause of Christ. At the same time, His patience and love for these people is remarkably obvious and often overlooked.

Right after Christ warns them of the possibility of spewing them out of His mouth, we see a tremendous amount of passion in Christ's letter. His compassion is easy to spot in these verses: "You say, 'I am rich. I have everything I want. I don't need a thing!' And you don't realize that you are wretched and miserable and poor and blind and naked. So, I advise you to buy gold from me—gold that has been purified by fire. Then you will be rich. Also buy white garments from me so you will not be shamed by your nakedness, and ointment for your eyes so you will be able to see. I correct and discipline everyone I love. So be diligent and turn from your indifference. "Look! I stand at the door and knock. If you hear my voice and open the door, I will come in, and we will share a meal together as friends. Those who are victorious will sit with me on my throne, just as I was victorious and sat with my Father on his throne." (Revelation 3:17-21, NLT). "You don't realize that you are wretched", Jesus says. He is trying to open their eyes to reality, passionately hoping that if they really see their own spiritual condition, they will take action to change it. "So I advise you..." Jesus says. He counsels them to focus their attention on the eternal things they can get from Him rather than the things they can purchase with their own wealth. "I correct and discipline everyone I love", He goes on to say. It is so reminiscent of John 15:9-10: "I have loved you even as the Father has loved me. Remain in my love. When you obey my commandments, you remain in my love, just as I obey my Father's commandments and remain in his love." (John 15:9-10, NLT). Jesus wants them to fix this problem so badly. He doesn't want to cut them off. He is giving them every opportunity to turn off the cold and turn up the hot in their relationship with Him.

Finally, Jesus ends with a word picture that blows me away. It is a verse we often use for evangelism purposes, but Jesus is saying this to the church. These words are given initially to Christians. They smack of passion for the wayward church. "Look! I stand at the door and knock. If you hear my voice and open the door, I will come in, and we will share a meal together as friends." The imagery is so sad. It is as if the church is inside their meeting place. They may be singing great Christian hymns or choruses. They may have their hands raised in worship. They are listening to a preacher expound the Word of God. But Jesus is on the outside of the door knocking. He is peering through the glass doors watching it all happen. It all looks so good and pious, but it is void of any spiritual life. He isn't any part of any of their Christian activity. He is on the outside looking in. He longs to be a part of it, but the church is too busy with its forms and its rituals to even notice. To be cut off, or spit from the mouth of God is not a decision God initiates. It is a response to the decision of men and women. It is a response to the decision of the church.

John 15 ends with a plea from Jesus to remain in Him, and to remain in His love. He calls on us to avoid falling into form, ritual, and lifeless Christianity. He petitions us to be filled with His life and power, and to use that to be fruit bearing believers. Then He gives us the litmus test. He tells us that we remain in His love when we obey His commands. If we start with the following two we will never be cold Christians. If we start here, we will never stop bearing fruit. If we obey these fully, we will never need to fear being cut off or cast away. "You must love the LORD your God with all your heart, all your soul, and all your mind. This is the first and greatest commandment. A second is equally important: 'Love your neighbour as yourself." (Matthew 22:37-39, NLT).

John 15 is a stern warning. There is no doubt about that. But it is a warning attached to a loving plea. It is a warning against setting up wrong priorities. It is a warning against becoming cold and lifeless. It is a warning against having a form of godliness, yet without power to live a godly life. It is a warning against trying to bear fruit without tapping into Him as your life source. It is a warning against living a life that is contradictory to your testimony. If you choose to live by wrong priorities, if you choose to be lukewarm in your walk with Him, if you choose to live a powerless and lifeless religious existence – then you leave God with no choice. You are choosing to be cut off. That is if you don`t wither away first, and be cast aside to be burned in the fire. It's all up to you. He responds to your choice.

10 A BUNCH MORE FRUIT

The things that Jesus did during three short years of ministry were remarkable. Apart from teaching and preaching with an authority that could only come from heaven, and revealing the very nature of God through His character, He also showed the power of God to the world in incredible ways. An immeasurable number of people were healed. He cast out demons. He turned water into wine, walked on water, calmed a storm, and fed multitudes with next to no food. It is recorded that Jesus raised three people from the dead. Those are things that we know, but John said: "Jesus also did many other things. If they were all written down, I suppose the whole world could not contain the books that would be written." (John 21:25, NLT)

Jesus Works

Then He left. Before He left, He said two very important things. First, He said: "I tell you the truth, anyone who believes in me will do the same works I have done, and even greater works, because I am going to be with the Father. You can ask for anything in my name, and I will do it, so that the Son can bring glory to the Father. Yes, ask me for anything in my name, and I will do it!" (John 14:12-14, NLT). We must travel down a quick bunny trail while discussing these verses to correct the misapplication that so often takes place.

To ask for something in Jesus' Name is to ask for something that is completely aligned with His will. These verses do not give license to use the Name of Jesus as part of a Christian incantation that will obligate God to give us whatever we want. To ask in His Name means that we are doing His business, for His purposes, and for His glory. We must understand verses 13 and 14 in their context. The topic at hand is doing the things that Jesus had been doing, even in greater measure. Jesus did not perform one selfish act. He lived completely for the purpose of revealing and glorifying the Father, and leading people to Him. That defines the purpose for which we can use the Name of Jesus authoritatively. You can't take your company credit card with the company's name on it and use it for whatever you want. That would get you fired rather quickly. When you use it for company purposes, however, you have great resources available to you. When we approach the Father in the Name of Jesus, we need to be careful to not come with selfish requests. We come to do business for Jesus.

Can modern day Christians really do the work of Christ? If we think of Christ as the head, and the church as His body on earth, we can only answer with a resounding "Yes". Christ remains on this earth through His body. Of course, we can do what He did.

Witness Works

The second prophecy of Jesus that we will consider is this: "But you will receive power when the Holy Spirit comes upon you. And you will be my witnesses, telling people about me everywhere—in Jerusalem, throughout Judea, in Samaria, and to the ends of the earth." (Acts 1:8, NLT). When we put these verses together, Jesus says that because He is going to the Father He will send us the Holy Spirit so that we will have both authority and power to do His work. Most importantly we will be powerful witnesses so that we can bear even more fruit. If we come to a full understanding of these verses Jesus taught us that we, the church, will do the same things He did – no, even greater things and in greater quantity. I don't know about you, but this thought does two things to me. It creates a longing in my spirit to bear that kind of fruit. I want to do what Jesus did, and I want to do it for His purposes and glory. Everything Christian within me cries out for this kind of effective ministry. At the same time, it stirs up feelings of insufficiency. I feel every ounce of frailty in my humanity. I remember my sins. My feeble mind tells me that this could only amount to a pipe dream. It tells me that this prophecy must be for the relative few super-Christians out there. The early church proved Christ's prediction to be both possible and true, and feelings of insufficiency to be a mere excuse.

Before we look at the accomplishments of the early church, let's give some thought to a couple of truths fundamental to this topic. We will consider the word "witness" first, as it was used in Acts 1:8. Jesus said that we will be His witnesses. The Greek word used here is 'martus' (pronounced 'mar-toos'). In the Scripture it is translated "witness" twenty-nine times. It is translated 'martyr' three times. Witness is a legal term used for someone who can give credible testimony to what they have seen or experienced. Since the word can also be translated 'martyr' we understand the lengths to which some have gone to stand up as a witness for what they have personally seen and experienced in their relationship with Jesus. They are so certain of God and His Word that they are willing to lay their lives down for it. This should take our minds back to the sixth chapter. The reason we don't experience the fullness of God's power is because we haven't fully crucified the flesh. We haven't martyred the flesh. We haven't become so certain of God's Word and His promises to us that we are willing to completely eradicate our selfish desires for the sake of proving the reality of God`s love and power. This suggests that there are limits to our faith which places limits on our ability to witness. We may say the right words, but part of witnessing has to be acting like we truly believe in God`s unlimited ability and His desire to reveal it through us. According to Jesus that means believing that we can do the things that He did. Is what you have seen and experienced of God real enough to build that kind of faith in you? Only then can we accomplish what He truly wants to accomplish through us.

Why, Jesus? Why?

To understand what He wants to accomplish through us we must also re-consider the things that Jesus did. Immediately our minds go to the miracles, healings, and even raising people from the dead. We think of walking on water and feeding the masses, just as I mentioned earlier. Certainly Jesus did those things, and it is very possible that the same Spirit could do those things through us. Ultimately, however, His purpose was to reveal the nature of God. That is what the healings, miracles, etc. were all about. He wanted the world to see the omniscience and omnipotence of God in action. He wanted them to experience His love and compassion. He wanted them to be certain that this world is God's Kingdom, and that even wind, waves, water, sickness, demons, and death must obey God, the King. God`s desire for the church today is that we reveal the Kingdom of God in this same way to the world around us. In the end, Jesus built a bridge between sinful man and our Creator. It was a bridge over the impassable cavern caused by man`s sin. That has been completed by Jesus. We can do all the other things Jesus did to draw people to Him. We can reveal the nature of God, His love, His compassion, and the nature of His Kingdom. Our ability to do the work of Jesus flows out of an absolute certainty that He is alive today and that His chosen means of continuing to reveal the nature of God is through us.

Baby Fruit

Earlier I wrote that "the early church proved Christ's prediction to be both possible and true, and feelings of insufficiency to be a mere excuse." We do fight against our personal insecurities. Not only that, in some cases you have an argument with the theology you have been brought up with, as well as lack of evidence. Not many have commonly seen the power of God at work through the church as it happened in the early chapters of Acts. But it did happen! Not having seen it in your personal past is not an excuse for not believing that it can happen through you in the present. Unless you believe that the Spirit of God has become old and powerless, you have to believe that what happened in those early days of the church can happen today.

Let's consider some of the things that happened in the early days of the baby church. Peter preached, three thousand people were pricked in their hearts and begged to know what they had to do to become followers of Christ. "A deep sense of awe came over them all, and the apostles performed many miraculous signs and wonders. And all the believers met together in one place and shared everything they had. They sold their property and possessions and shared the money with those in need. They worshiped together at the Temple each day, met in homes for the Lord's Supper, and shared their meals with great joy and generosity— all the while praising God and enjoying the goodwill of all the people. And each day the Lord added to their fellowship those who were being saved." (Acts 2:43-47, NLT). Miracles, signs and wonders were common. They led to a sense of awe, resulting in people coming to know Christ by the day.

A man who was lame from birth caught Peter and John's attention at the temple gate. They had probably passed by this man many times. Begging was the way he made his living. It was the only means he had to get some food. He was taken to the same place each day for this purpose. This time, however, Peter and John's pockets were empty. They had no money to offer him. That's all he wanted; just a little cash so that he could have someone run down to the local deli for him and purchase a bologna sandwich and a cup of coffee. Faith stirred in Peter, however. "I don't have any silver or gold for you. But I'll give you what I have. In the name of Jesus Christ the Nazarene, get up and walk!" (Acts 3:6, NLT). What Peter had was the Spirit of God. What he had was authority in the Name of Jesus to do what Jesus had done. Peter was just a man. He had more reason to feel weak and insecure than most of us. He was just an uneducated fisherman from Galilee who had previously disappointed Jesus on numerous occasions. But now he was full of the Holy Spirit. Things were different.

Listen to this: "more and more people believed and were brought to the Lord—crowds of both men and women. As a result of the apostles' work, sick people were brought out into the streets on beds and mats so that

Peter's shadow might fall across some of them as he went by. Crowds came from the villages around Jerusalem, bringing their sick and those possessed by evil spirits, and they were all healed." (Acts 5:14-16, NLT). Wow! When people who had a sick, diseased, or physically disabled person in their home saw Peter coming they would quickly find a way to get their loved one to the street. The street would be lined with people stretched out on beds and mats. They were certain that if they were so fortunate that Peter's shadow might fall on their loved one, they would be healed. The sick and demon possessed were brought to Jerusalem from all over. They were all healed. Even the dead were raised, just as Jesus had done. Acts chapter 9 records the raising of Tabitha from the dead. They were doing it! They were doing the work that Jesus did, and people were being added to the family of God en mass.

It wasn't just Peter doing this. "Philip, for example, went to the city of Samaria and told the people there about the Messiah. Crowds listened intently to Philip because they were eager to hear his message and see the miraculous signs he did. Many evil spirits were cast out, screaming as they left their victims. And many who had been paralyzed or lame were healed. So, there was great joy in that city." (Acts 5:5-8, NLT).

Here is the thing. The same Spirit that lived in Peter lives in you and me today. The same Spirit that lived in Philip lives in us. He is not old. He is not powerless. It is not Him that has changed. It is us. It is the church. We can do the work of Christ today because the same Spirit is alive and well, and living in us. We must keep in mind that we don't seek after the supernatural for the sake of seeing the supernatural. It is not the supernatural we worship or serve, it is God. We seek to show the world that God is real, powerful, and loving. If God chooses to do that through the supernatural, which He has done historically, we need to have faith to be used for His glory. It was in this atmosphere where signs, wonders, miracles, and healing took place that the church grew from 120 to thousands in a matter of days. Now, that's fruit.

Proven Potency

Just in case you believe that this power was only for the apostles, think again. Paul prayed that the Christians in Ephesus have this same kind of power. "I also pray that you will understand the incredible greatness of God's power for us who believe him. This is the same mighty power that raised Christ from the dead and seated him in the place of honour at God's right hand in the heavenly realms. Now he is far above any ruler or authority or power or leader or anything else—not only in this world but also in the world to come." (Ephesians 1:19-21, NLT). These verses deserve a little attention.

Paul prays that the Christians understand the incredible greatness of God's power that is for us who believe. The New International Version of the Bible calls it: "incomparably great power". This power resides in God by virtue of His very nature. God, in turn, dwells in us by His Holy Spirit which makes it possible for this power to flow through us. It is 'dunamis' (Gk) power, or dynamic power. It is an undeniable ability to perform a task. To prove His point, Paul directs our thoughts to the resurrection of Jesus from the dead. If God can do that He is clearly capable of completing whatever task He takes on. But let us not forget that Paul is trying to drive home the point that this incredibly great power is available to those who believe in Him. We can tap into God's power to do God's work for God's purposes. It is incredible power. It is incomparable power. It is great power. It is Divine power. If as Christians we believe that God dwells in our hearts by His Holy Spirit, which was made possible by the work of Christ at Calvary, we must never limit God's ability to do His work through us. Not by our lack of faith. Not because of lack of understanding. Not by our lack of willingness to be used. Not by choosing to live a lifestyle that does not reflect His nature. We must not allow anything to get in the way of God's great power flowing through us to bear fruit for His glory.

We commonly uphold the likes of Elijah and Elisha as being great men of God. We do that because God did great wonders and miracles through them. After all, Elijah called down fire from heaven. He was miraculously ushered into heaven by way of a chariot of fire. Elisha made bitter water sweet, caused a bottle of oil to fill many jars, raised the Shunammites's son from the dead, and fed 100 men with 20 loaves of barley bread. This is just to mention a few of the things that God did through these men. We look at Moses and are at awe of some of the miracles God did through Him. He parted the sea, and caused water to flow from rocks. These are remarkable things. James made a statement regarding Elijah that pertains to them all: "Elijah was as human as we are, and yet when he prayed earnestly that no rain would fall, none fell for three and a half years! Then, when he prayed again, the sky sent down rain and the earth began to yield its crops." (James 5:17-18, NLT). Elijah, Elisha, and Moses were human, just as we are. They put their sandals on one foot at a time. What they didn't have was the kind of intimate relationship that we have with the Holy Spirit. The Old Testament saints had a completely external relationship with God. God was with them, but they did not have the Holy Spirit dwelling in them as we do. That was made possible through the death, resurrection and ascension of Jesus. So, they were ordinary humans who had a less intimate relationship with God than we do, whom God used to do remarkable things. That being the case, why do we have a difficult time believing that God can work through us Spirit filled believers to do the things Jesus did in order to reveal the glory, love and power of God to the world? The Spirit of God dwells in us for this very purpose. We have no excuse. God dwells in us. We are the temple of His Holy Spirit. We are His body on earth. We simply need to come to an understanding of His incredibly great power and begin to allow it to flow through us to bear bunches of fruit for His glory and the growth of His Kingdom.

It is time for the church to take God at His Word. It is time for us to believe that we will and should be doing the things that Jesus did, for the same purpose and with the same motive. We need to be ready to be used when and how the Spirit of God wants to use us. It is time for us to believe that we have God's incredibly great power available to us, to be His witnesses, no matter what it costs.

A Holy Spirit Gift Basket

The apostle Paul gives even more specific teaching on the availability of the Holy Spirit in his letter to the Corinthians. He speaks of gifts that are resident in the Holy Spirit that He will impart to Christian believers. They are supernatural gifts. They are gifts that enable us to know, understand, believe, and accomplish things that are beyond human ability. There are nine of them.

As we've already discussed, the three years of Jesus ministry were marked with the supernatural. What we so often forget is that during this time He laid the rights and power of His Divinity aside. He left Divine attributes behind when He left His home in heaven. He didn't stop being God, but He came to earth to be fully human and to fully experience humanity. To accomplish the things that Jesus did, He was operating in the power and leading of the Holy Spirit. Luke makes this very clear when he records the very beginning of Jesus' ministry. In Luke 4:1 we read that Jesus, after His baptism, was full of the Holy Spirit. He was then led by the Spirit into the desert of temptation. In verse 14 he returned to Galilee in the power of the Holy Spirit. The difference between Jesus and us was that He was not obstructed by sin or selfishness. Though He was fully human He was not born in sin like the rest of us. Nor did He commit acts of sin like the rest of us. In addition to this, His life was completely motivated by His desire to do the will of the Father and to reveal Him to mankind. Long before Jesus was crucified at Calvary, He crucified Himself. He put His flesh to death. He was completely dead to selfish desires and sin. A look at Jesus' life and ministry reveals that the gifts of the Holy Spirit were consistently at work through Him. That same power that He operated in is available to us today. The more we die to sin and self, the more able we are to minister in the power of the Holy Spirit.

These are the gifts of the Holy Spirit that Paul listed: "To one person the Spirit gives the ability to give wise advice; to another the same Spirit gives a message of special knowledge. The same Spirit gives great faith to another, and to someone else the one Spirit gives the gift of healing. He gives one person the power to perform miracles, and another the ability to prophesy. He gives someone else the ability to discern whether a message is from the Spirit of God or from another spirit. Still another person is given the ability to speak in unknown languages, while another is given the ability to interpret what is being said. It is the one and only Spirit who distributes all these gifts. He alone decides which gift each person should have." (1 Corinthians 12:8-11, NLT). The gifts of the Holy Spirit are:

- The gift of wisdom
- The gift of knowledge
- The gift of faith
- The gift of healing
- The gift of miracles
- The gift of discerning of spirits
- The gift of prophecy
- The gift of tongues
- The gift of interpretation of tongues

We have some of these things naturally. We all have some level of wisdom. We all have a degree of knowledge. Everyone puts their faith in something. But there is nothing natural about the gifts of the Holy Spirit.

Paul is speaking of a supernatural wisdom that is rooted in the mind of God, whose thoughts are beyond our ability to understand except by the Holy Spirit. God said to Isaiah that "For just as the heavens are higher than the earth, so my ways are higher than your ways and my thoughts higher than your thoughts." (Isaiah 55:9, NLT). God sees things that we can`t see. He has a perspective that is impossible for us to have. He has a bird`s eye view of time: past, present, and future. He knows the beginning from the end. He knows our thoughts and emotions. He knows everything. Because of His perfect knowledge and perfect character His wisdom is flawless. When the Holy Spirit chooses to, He will impart to us a morsel of this godly wisdom to help us help ourselves or others. Don`t misunderstand. We could never be as wise as God. Still, through this gift, He will share His wisdom for a specific situation at a specific time.

Wisdom is the correct application of knowledge; but it always begins with knowledge. We serve an all-knowing God. He knows every detail of your life. According to Matthew 10:30, He even knows how many hairs you have on your head. He doesn't just know the number of hairs on your head, He knows everybody`s. That gives you a hint as to the depth of His knowledge. There are times when, by His Spirit, God will reveal appropriate knowledge to an individual that they could not have otherwise, to assist them in ministering to others.

There are times when the Spirit will enhance whatever faith you have for a situation and multiply it so that every core of your being is certain that God will move in power to supernaturally alter that circumstance. When this happens you know that you know that you know that you know God is at work. It doesn`t even seem like faith to you. Even though it hasn`t happened yet it is as good as substance to you because there is no shred of doubt. It is a done deal. This is not naivety, or presumption. This is the gift of faith that comes from God.

The power and desire of God to heal and to perform miracles is unquestionably proven in the New Testament. An extensive discussion on this topic, and how these gifts apply to our present day, has been the inspiration of many books in and of themselves. Can or will God heal today?

To answer the question with a "No" would suggest that Jesus has changed. The writer to the Hebrews said that: "Jesus Christ is the same yesterday, today, and forever." (Hebrews 13:8, NLT). So, the answer is "Yes." Our earlier assessment of the New Testament church is clear indication of the fact that God wants to use His church to continue His work in this way. Healings and miracles not only bless the recipient, but they draw attention to both the love and the power of God. They lift Him up. Where Christ is lifted up, people are drawn to Him. Immediately after Jesus' ascension into heaven, the disciples got busy. The Word says "the disciples went everywhere and preached, and the Lord worked through them, confirming what they said by many miraculous signs." (Mark 16:20, NTL). Healings and miracles not only benefit individuals, revealing God's love and power; they confirm the truth of God's Word.

Even Christians often live as if it is just us human beings on this earth. We forget about the realm beyond our normal ability to see. We forget about the fallen angels, or demonic spirits that are Satan's pawns to try to influence men. The Gospels reveal that they can cause symptoms that appear to be illness, disease, deaf ears, seizures, or insanity. Satan attempts to steal and destroy the blessings of God from His people. "He prowls around like a roaring lion, looking for someone to devour." (1 Peter 5:8, NLT). But he doesn't do it all on his own. He is incapable. He uses his evil companions to endeavour to achieve these wicked goals. Satan is the father of lies, and so it is necessary for us to be able to discern whether or not we are dealing with a demonic spirit. We also live our lives without often acknowledging that God has commissioned angelic beings to watch over us. "For he will order his angels to protect you wherever you go." (Psalms 91:11, NLT). We don't need to live with any kind of anxiety over this; we simply need to be aware that there are evil spirits, angelic spirits, human spirits, and God's Spirit. Fifty percent of those can act poorly and be deceptive. Paul wrote: "And I am convinced that nothing can ever separate us from God's love. Neither death nor life, neither angels nor demons, neither our fears for today nor our worries about tomorrow—not even the powers of hell can separate us from God's love." (Romans 8:38, NLT). When we are ministering to people, however, God may feel that it is important for you to know what kind of spirit you are dealing with. To increase the effectiveness of your ministry He may reveal that to you. For example, if you are ministering to someone who appears to be ill in their mind or body, but their symptoms are caused by a demonic spirit, you will deal with this differently. Praying for healing could prove futile. Telling the demon where to go would be very beneficial. It is very important for you to know what you are dealing with at times.

The vocal gifts of the Holy Spirit: prophecy, tongues and interpretation of tongues are more for the comfort, building up, and strengthening of the body of Christ. These gifts deliver a message from the heart and mind of God through believers that are sensitive carriers of that message. Paul makes clear, in his instructions regarding an orderly church service in 1 Corinthians 14, that these gifts have dual purpose. On one hand they are for the strengthening of the church, and on the other hand he says that that tongues and interpretation are a sign for the unbeliever, revealing God's presence. He also says that prophecy can convict the non-believer of sin. So, these gifts have fruit bearing value among both believers and unbelievers.

Here is a very important point. Couched between Paul's lesson on the gifts of the Holy Spirit and unity among believers in 1 Corinthians 12, and his teaching on conducting an orderly church service in chapter 14, is what we commonly refer to as 'the love chapter'. Paul is teaching us that if these gifts of the Holy Spirit are not the outcome of the fruit of the Holy Spirit, they are useless. They have no fruit-bearing value. As much as the purpose of these gifts is to bear fruit, they must be spiritual fruit of spiritual fruit – the fruit of the Holy Spirit. They must be born out of Christ-like character to be effective. It is otherwise impossible for them to bear godly fruit that builds up the kingdom of God. Spiritual power without character has no value to anyone. This is why Paul wrote: "If I could speak all the languages of earth and of angels, but didn't love others, I would only be a noisy gong or a clanging cymbal. If I had the gift of prophecy, and if I understood all of God's secret plans and possessed all knowledge, and if I had such faith that I could move mountains, but didn't love others, I would be nothing. If I gave everything I have to the poor and even sacrificed my body, I could boast about it; but if I didn't love others, I would have gained nothing." (1 Corinthians 13:1-3, NLT) The same author taught a reduced version of this truth to the Galatian Christians "What is important is faith expressing itself in love." (Galatians 5:6, NLT)

We must give serious consideration to one other important point relative to the gifts of the Holy Spirit. These gifts are not some kind of device that we turn on and off like a light switch. The Holy Spirit gives them to us as He wills. He does not give them so that we can impress people. They are not for our pleasure or for our glory. They are given for specific situations at specific times for God's purposes and His glory. There is no room for pride when God uses us through these gifts. It is God's power, not ours. It is to accomplish His will, not ours. It is to bear fruit for His Kingdom, not ours. When the apostle Philip was in Samaria soon after Pentecost he had a very effective evangelistic ministry, but none of them had received the Holy Spirit. Peter and John went on a road trip to see what God was doing there. What they found was awesome. Even a man named Simon, who had practiced sorcery, had accepted Christ and was baptized. He had been very popular because of the evil magic he could perform, but even He was astonished by the miracles and healings that were happening as Philip prayed. Having been one who always drew a crowd, Simon now followed Philip everywhere he went. When Peter and John arrived, they started laying hands on people, who then began to receive the baptism of the Holy Spirit. Now Simon was in complete awe. He lusted after the kind of power that Peter and John had. He wanted it so badly that he offered them money to be enabled to do what they were doing. Peter's response was rapid and direct: "May your money be destroyed with you for thinking God's gift can be bought! You can have no part in this, for your heart is not right with God. Repent of your wickedness and pray to the Lord. Perhaps he will forgive your evil thoughts, for I can see that you are full of bitter jealousy and are held captive by sin." (Acts 8:20-23, NLT)

It is appropriate to seek after the gifts of the Holy Spirit. Paul taught us to "Let love be your highest goal! But you should also desire the special abilities the Spirit gives—especially the ability to prophesy." (1 Corinthians 14:1, NLT). But your reason for doing so must be so that you can do the work of God with greater effectiveness, bearing much fruit. If you want the gifts so you can say that you've reached a new spiritual level, your motive is wrong. If you want the gifts to feel powerful, your motive is wrong. If you want the gifts to draw attention to yourself in any way, your motive is wrong. The gifts of the Holy Spirit are so that we can do the work Jesus did – even greater things for the sake of His Kingdom.

Jesus and the Gifts

Let's take a look at a few examples where the gifts of the Holy Spirit were at work in Jesus' ministry. Jesus was doing something that Jews did not commonly do. He was travelling through Samaria. Tired and thirsty, He sat down by an ancient well dug by the Jewish patriarch Jacob many hundreds of years before. We don't know the amount of time that passed before a Samaritan woman came along to draw water, or if many had come before her. Jesus asked if she would give Him a drink. After Jesus ministers to her in a very relevant and effective manner, offering her living water, this remarkable conversation takes place: "Go and get your husband," Jesus told her. "I don't have a husband," the woman replied. Jesus said, "You're right! You don't have a husband— 18 for you have had five husbands, and you aren't even married to the man you're living with now. You certainly spoke the truth!" (John 4:16-18, NLT). Jesus knew things that could only be known supernaturally, and He ministered with uncanny wisdom. The gifts of knowledge and of wisdom were definitely at work here.

Jesus' good friends, Mary and Martha, sent word to Him that their brother Lazarus was very ill. Jesus responded almost as if He knew already: "Lazarus's sickness will not end in death. No, it happened for the glory of God so that the Son of God will receive glory from this." (John 11:14, NLT). Without any further messages from the sisters, Jesus later said: "Our friend Lazarus has fallen asleep, but now I will go and wake him up." The disciples said, "Lord, if he is sleeping, he will soon get better!" They thought Jesus meant Lazarus was simply sleeping, but Jesus meant Lazarus had died. So he told them plainly, "Lazarus is dead. And for your sakes, I'm glad I wasn't there, for now you will really believe. Come, let's go see him." (John 11:11-15, NLT). When they finally arrived in Bethany, where Mary, Martha, and Lazarus lived, Jesus' friend had been dead four days. After a very emotional trip to the tomb, this happened: "Roll the stone aside," Jesus told them. But Martha, the dead man's sister, protested, "Lord, he has been dead for four days. The smell will be terrible." Jesus responded, "Didn't I tell you that you would see God's glory if you believe?" So they rolled the stone aside. Then Jesus looked up to heaven and said, "Father, thank you for hearing me. You always hear me, but I said it out loud for the sake of all these people standing here, so that they will believe you sent me." Then Jesus shouted, "Lazarus, come out!" And the dead man came out, his hands and feet bound in graveclothes, his face wrapped in a headcloth. Jesus told them, "Unwrap him and let him go!" (John 11:39-44, NLT). Before being told, Jesus knew about Lazarus' sickness. Without getting word, Jesus knew when Lazarus died. He had wisdom to not go to Bethany while Lazarus was still alive to bring greater glory to the Father. Finally, he raised Lazarus from the dead. We see the gifts of knowledge, wisdom, faith, and miracles all working together. "Many of the people who were with Mary believed in Jesus when they saw this happen. (John 11:45, NLT). There was great fruit.

The gospels are filled with stories about the ministry of Jesus. What we often don't realize is that the gospels are equally filled with stories about the ministry of the Holy Spirit. What Jesus, the man, did on earth He did by the power of the Holy Spirit. His supernatural knowledge came from the Holy Spirit. His supernatural wisdom came from the Holy Spirit. His ability to discern and cast out spirits came from the Holy Spirit. His great faith and power to perform miracles and heal every kind of disease came from the Holy Spirit. It wasn't that Jesus, the Son of God, didn't have those abilities. It was that He left them behind in heaven so that He could experience manhood fully. So everything Jesus did, He did through the power of the Holy Spirit.

Then He left. He immediately sent that same Spirit to live in us, with the instruction to do the same things He had been doing – even greater things. He sent that same Spirit to empower us to be His witnesses. He established the church as His body on earth. Jesus is very much present here through the church. If we would allow our character to be transformed into the likeness of Christ, His power would be able to flow through us so freely. If we would use that power to be His witnesses there would be so much fruit. If we would use His power to do His work, there is no reason why today's church wouldn't be as effective as the church we read about in Acts 2 through 10. Wouldn't it be awesome for signs and wonders to consistently confirm the power, love, and Word of God where you live? Wouldn't it be amazing for the church to be added to daily in your community? The Holy Spirit hasn't changed. The church has.

11 THE TESTIMONY OF GOD THROUGH YOU

The Biblically, evangelism didn't take place in a church building. Nobody rented a stadium. The city wasn't blanketed with tracts. There were no evangelistic programs. I'm not against any of those things. It's just not the way it was done in the New Testament. It was the ministry of individuals bearing the fruit of the Holy Spirit, living pure lives, sharing their love for Jesus, and witnessing in His power. Signs and wonders regularly confirmed His Word. This is what caused such amazing church growth.

In the 21st century church, if there isn't consistent church growth, many people sit back in their pew and accuse the church leadership of not doing enough. They evaluate the church programs and determine that they are not being run effectively. If they were, more new people would be brought into the church. This societal shift among Christian believers must shift back. Fruit bearing is not the responsibility of the church organization; it is the responsibility of every part that makes up the whole. Every member of the body of Christ must be actively involved in doing it, not directing it.

This is why the church needs revival today. This revival must be both personal and corporate. It is not about having exciting services, great worship, or an emotional moment at the altar. The very word revival suggests life had, life lost, and life regained. In my opinion, the time that the church was most full of life was the time period recorded in Acts chapters 2 through 10. I say that because of its amazing effectiveness. I say it because of the great harvest of fruit that took place. We've lost that kind of spiritual vitality and must get it back. You need to take personal responsibility for making that happen. So do I. The church is, and has always been, a collection of individuals. Corporate revival resulting in a bountiful harvest of fruit will come when we all determine that we will become an 'Acts' kind of Christian.

Fruit Loose Summary

To some degree, this entire book has been about that. It has been about life had, life lost, and how to regain it. It has been about revival. This is an appropriate time to review what we've discussed about changing our personal behaviour in order to become an effective, fruit-bearing believer.

1. We must strive to achieve a Christ-like character. This will come only as we submit ourselves to the work of the Holy Spirit, who will enable us to bear the fruit of Christ's character. We must also bear the fruit of righteousness. The end goal of both of these achievements is that we bear the fruit of souls for the growth of God's kingdom.

2. We must stop starving our spirits and feed on those things that will build us up and strengthen our spirit man. When we don't, we tend to experience malnutrition in our spirits. It is then that we tend to become spiritually lethargic, or even hurtful to others around us rather than bearing fruit. When we spend time feeding on God's

Word and presence, we have His life flowing through us to become effective, fruit bearing Christians.

3. Because the church is the body of Christ with Him as our head, we must be collectively driven by the desire to reveal His nature, do the same work, and fulfil the same purpose that Jesus did. We may be able to manufacture many excuses for not doing that, but the reality is that Christ is with us and lives in us to enable us to do these things.

4. The title of Christian bears great responsibility. We must take a pure gospel into the streets. That pure gospel must be reflected in our lifestyle. If not, our attempt at witnessing may cause more harm than good. When we take our responsibility as Christians seriously our words and our lifestyle will be in alignment. Then we can be remarkably effective in doing the work of Christ.

5. Christ is the anointed one and He lives in us by His Holy Spirit. That means that when we are committed to fulfilling His purposes, we can be sure that His anointing will flow through us to do His work and to bear much fruit for His glory.

6. For Christ's anointing to be able to flow through us without obstruction, we must die completely to everything within us that is attached to temporal values and selfish goals. Only then can we truly reflect His character and not ours. Only then can we be effective fruit bearing Christians.

7. Unity means that everyone in the church is moving in the same direction, at the same time, for the same purpose. That is how any 'body' works. It is how a 'body' gets from point A to point B. No one person can take responsibility for fruit bearing in any community. Neither can any single church. It is the responsibility of the whole body of Christ and all of its members to work together for this one purpose.

8. It is quite natural for us to have comfort zones in which we will minister. The lines that define those comfort zones must be removed. We must abandon ourselves to ministering in whatever place and in whatever way the Holy Spirit leads us. To be effective fruit-bearers there can be no such thing as "limits" in our willingness to serve God in any place, to any person, or at any time.

9. Christ made it very clear that those Christians who do not bear fruit are in danger of being cut off from Him. He will also take steps to prune those that are. Both of these measures are to increase the effectiveness of the church. This is a very stern Scriptural warning to take the message of fruit bearing seriously.

10. The power of the Holy Spirit is available to us to do His work today. The nature of that power as well as the nature of the work that He does is revealed through the life of Jesus and the early church as recorded in the book of Acts.

It doesn't seem like it should be that hard. It doesn't seem like these things are difficult. The benefits to the lost world around us, and the personal benefit of knowing that we have served God in the way that He desires is well worth the effort to any serious believer.

Posturing To Be an 'Acts' Kind of Christian

Most mature Christians will read this book and agree with a large percentage of it. In fact many have either heard or thought of lots of these things before, but perhaps not in a compilation like this, or in the context of fruit-bearing. Still, as much as you agree, the impact of these truths has had minimal effect to date. For as long as you have known these things, these principles have had little impact on your life. Truthfully, your life is bearing little fruit of eternal value. Why is that? Why can we give mental assent to Biblical truths and sincerely desire to follow Biblical principles, and yet never do it? It is because desire and intellectual assent are not enough. We must put ourselves in a spiritual position, or posture, where God can help us do the things we say "yes" to. These are spiritual principles that require God's strength and support. They are an act of our will, but require the impetus of the Holy Spirit for them to be achievable. The apostle Paul wrote the secret to this: "And so, dear brothers and sisters, I plead with you to give your bodies to God because of all he has done for you. Let them be a living and holy sacrifice—the kind he will find acceptable. This is truly the way to worship him. Don't copy the behavior and customs of this world, but let God transform you into a new person by changing the way you think. Then you will learn to know God's will for you, which is good and pleasing and perfect." (Romans 12:1-2, NLT). What strikes me here is that we have a significant part to play in receiving all that the Spirit of God has for us. He does the real work, but we have to put ourselves in a position where He can do it. We must be willing to lay down who we are in order that God can raise us up as the pure and powerful person He wants us to be.

Lay Down Natural Abilities to Make Room for Spiritual Abilities

The apostle Paul learned this lesson the hard way. When he was young, he had a different name. His name was Saul. He was a man with great promise. He had received the best education in Jewish law. He was a very religious Pharisee. He had a great sociological advantage in that he held both Jewish and Roman citizenship. Besides all this, he had a level of intelligence that surpassed most.

The problem was that Saul hated Christians. He was not only present when Stephen was stoned in the early days of the church, he was there checking coats. He was actively involved. "His accusers took off their coats and laid them at the feet of a young man named Saul." (Acts 7:58, NLT). The Word goes on to say that "Saul was one of the witnesses, and he agreed completely with the killing of Stephen. A great wave of persecution began that day, sweeping over the church in Jerusalem; and all the believers except the apostles were scattered through the regions of Judea and Samaria. (Some devout men came and buried Stephen with great mourning.) But Saul was going everywhere to destroy the church. He went from house to house, dragging out both men and women to throw them into prison." (Acts 8:1-3, NLT). Saul went so far as to get a letter from the High Priest, giving him permission to go to Damascus and bring back to Jerusalem all the Christians he could find, both men and women, to receive their punishment. Saul had become a leader in the persecution of Christian believers.

Saul was getting close to Damascus when God apprehended him. A light from heaven flashed around him. He fell to the ground, and the glorified Christ spoke to him. He asked Saul why he was persecuting Him. It seemed a little drastic, but God was putting Saul in a place where He could change, empower, and use him for His glory.

Saul became the Apostle Paul. He wrote 13 or 14 of the 27 books of the New Testament. Countless churches in numerous countries were started as a result of Paul's evangelistic endeavours. Not only was his name changed, everything about him was changed. He completely laid down everything he was before God as a living sacrifice, and said "use me".

To be used of God in a significant way, we must be willing to look inside of ourselves and find those things about our own personalities that we trust in more than God. We must find those things that we turn to before we turn to Him. Whatever you use to influence people around you other than the Holy Spirit must go. It may be intellect, your skill set, artistic or musical talents, your personal charisma, persuasive abilities, or sociological advantage. God can, and likely will, use those things, but it can't be them that you rely on. Your confidence must rest in the Holy Spirit. Every one of those things must get knocked to the ground in the presence of God. You must actively lay them down as a sacrifice before God. Then, and only then, can He use your life to radically change the world around you.

Redirect the Strength of your Will to Obtain the Blessings of God

Jacob was a wealthy man. He had become that way largely through trickery and deceit. Genesis 32 tells the story of him returning to his home land from his Uncle Laban's home in Paddan Aram. He would soon meet his brother, Esau, who had vowed to kill him years before. That was, of course, because Jacob had stolen his birthright through trickery and deceit. At least he was consistent. He was returning with his two wives, Leah and Rachel, along with their children. He also had huge herds of livestock and camels, as well as flocks of fowl.

He had so many animals that he was able to send 200 female goats, 20 male goats, 200 ewes, 20 rams, 30 female camels with their young, 40 cows, 10 bulls, 20 female donkeys, and 10 male donkeys ahead as a gift to his brother. That barely put a dent in all that he had. There is no question about Jacob's success.

He divided his travel companions and the remaining animals into two groups. It was good strategy. If his brother attacked, then at least one group could escape. His wives and eleven children stayed with him until nightfall. He then sent them across the stream and he stayed alone. It was dark. God came. He came in the form of a man, and they had a physical wrestling match. It was a very strange situation, yet typical of our relationship with God. It was typical in the sense that Jacob was able to keep God from overpowering him by the sheer strength of his will. Clearly God could overcome Jacob physically if He chose. After all He disabled him, wrenching his hip with the mere touch of his finger. But, God could not overpower Jacob's will to win. That is the way God set our relationship in place from the beginning of time. He will not violate our will. He desires that we choose to serve Him.

Something other than the physical effect happened when God touched Jacob's hip. The power of Jacob's will was still strong, but he used the strength of his will very differently. It seems that his hip was wrenched and the light came on simultaneously. That was the whole point of this struggle. Suddenly the battle was no longer about self-preservation. It was no longer about self-protection. Jacob was now using this inner strength to acquire the blessing of God. "Then the man said, "Let me go, for the dawn is breaking!" But Jacob said, "I will not let you go unless you bless me." "What is your name?" the man asked. He replied, "Jacob." "Your name will no longer be Jacob," the man told him. "From now on you will be called Israel, because you have fought with God and with men and have won." (Gen. 32:26-28, NLT). Jacob's name was changed because his character changed at that very moment. He was changed from a deceiver to a prince with God.

Here is the lesson. Sometimes, even in our attempt to allow the Holy Spirit to transform, empower, and fill us with His love, it becomes a wrestling match. For those things to happen we must use the strength of our will to attain His will. We must give up the wrestling match we so often have, and simply say: "Bless me by using me!" We cannot say: "God, make me more like you", then say "It's okay, I'll do it myself". We cannot say: "God, give me your power to do your work and be your witness on earth.", and then say "It's okay, I can serve you in my own strength." The struggle we have within our self too often keeps us from allowing God to change and empower us. If we want to be an 'Acts' kind of Christian we must use the strength of our will to say "I will not let you go until you transform me, empower me, bless me, and use me for your glory."

Lay down All Claims to Glory, and Give it All to Him

Nebuchadnezzar was the king of Babylon; a great world empire. The empire flourished under his leadership. Daniel, Shadrach, Meshach, and Abednego were all exiles from Israel to Babylon at this time. Nebuchadnezzar had a dream that Daniel interpreted. It was an unpleasant prophecy that was fulfilled a year later. "Twelve months later he was taking a walk on the flat roof of the royal palace in Babylon. As he looked out across the city, he said, 'Look at this great city of Babylon! By my own mighty power, I have built this beautiful city as my royal residence to display my majestic splendor.' "While these words were still in his mouth, a voice called down from heaven, 'O King Nebuchadnezzar, this message is for you! You are no longer ruler of this kingdom. You will be driven from human society. You will live in the fields with the wild animals, and you will eat grass like a cow. Seven periods of time will pass while you live this way, until you learn that the Most High rules over the kingdoms of the world and gives them to anyone he chooses.' "That same hour the judgment was fulfilled, and Nebuchadnezzar was driven from human society. He ate grass like a cow, and he was drenched with the dew of heaven. He lived this way until his hair was as long as eagles' feathers and his nails were like birds' claws." (Daniel 4:29-33, NLT).

It seems that this is a different level or type of pride than what Saul struggled with. To some degree pride is pride, but it can manifest itself differently. Saul was confident in his own abilities and didn't recognize God as the source. Nebuchadnezzar was confident in his accomplishments as well, but he went so far as to set himself up as one to be looked at. Like Saul, he didn't feel a need for God, but he almost saw himself as one to be revered.

This is such an important lesson if we want to be effective witnesses for Jesus. Christ Himself taught that those who lift themselves up with pride are the least favoured. "He sat down, called the twelve disciples over to him, and said, "Whoever wants to be first must take last place and be the servant of everyone else." (Mark 9:35,

NLT). Understand that the power He gives us is not to draw attention to ourselves, but to enable us to be better servants of Him and those around us. We need to be empowered to serve others because the sinful flesh typically chooses to be self-serving. We need to be strengthened to humbly serve God, because humility often doesn't come naturally. Nothing will prevent the release of God's power into your life more effectively than a 'look at me' attitude. When you find yourselves saying, or even thinking "Look what I did!" you are in danger of being cut off from Christ's anointing. It is those that are humble that God can use. It is the humble that God recognizes as being great in the Kingdom of God. "But those who exalt themselves will be humbled, and those who humble themselves will be exalted." (Matthew 23:12, NLT)

The story of Shadrach, Meshach, and Abednego is known to almost everyone. God miraculously kept them safe in the midst of a fiery furnace. This happened under Nebuchadnezzar's reign prior to him going insane because of his pride. After the miracle, Nebuchadnezzar praised the God of Shadrach, Meshach, and Abednego. He acknowledged that no other god could have done this. He even decreed that if anyone says anything bad against their God he would have them cut into pieces and have their houses turned into a pile of rubble. That's a pretty effective evangelistic tool right there. Nebuchadnezzar acknowledged God's greatness, but his verbal acknowledgment of this wasn't enough. His spiritual posture was still one of pride.

If you want to experience God's power at work through you; if you want a greater release of Christ's anointing through you, you will have a clear vision of how small you are without Him. You will acknowledge your inability to accomplish anything if it weren't for the talents and abilities He has given you. You will humbly serve His people in His power without any hope of recognition and will give Him all the glory for whatever is accomplished. When you reach that place in all sincerity, you can expect an explosion of His power to be released through you to accomplish His work.

Laying down your natural abilities to attain the Spirit's Divine abilities, using the strength of your will to obtain His blessings, and making certain that your heart is clear of all pride is the spiritual posture God needs you to take to make you an 'Acts' kind of Christian. That is what it means to lay yourself down as a living sacrifice. Until you do this, people will only see you when you try to minister. They will appreciate what 'you' do. They will be impressed by 'your' wisdom. They will like your sermon, or your song, or your testimony, or appreciate the kind deed you did. But, when you offer yourself as a living sacrifice, everything about your life will point to God. People will see His wisdom in you. They will hear His message through your words. When you sing, they will hear a new song put in your heart by God. Your testimony will not be one about self, but about the grace of our Lord. Even the smallest act of kindness that you perform will point people to Jesus. When you take a posture of self-sacrifice, you can expect an 'Acts' kind of power to be released through your life; you can expect to do the works Jesus did, and you can expect to bear much eternal fruit for His Kingdom.

Practicalities

Now that we know how to posture ourselves to become all that God wants us to be so that we can bear all the fruit we can bear for God's glory, let's look at some practical ways that we can share the love of Jesus with others.

This is not a text book on how to pray for the sick, demonology, or evangelism. Praying for the sick and dealing with demons seems like it should be simple to me. Once we get the biblical principles we have discussed down pat, we merely pray in the Name of Jesus and in the authority of that Name. It is our level of faith, and our relationship with Him that is of prime importance. There is no magic formula. Evangelism is different; although faith, lifestyle, and relationship with God are still of vital importance. The work of the Holy Spirit is always the most important element to successful evangelism. To some degree, however, our ability to be effective is increased by understanding the uniqueness of the individual or culture we are ministering to.

I am a firm believer that the most effective means of evangelism in our western culture is through relationships. There is still a place for mass evangelistic services, television and radio programs, evangelistic events and programs at our churches, and even street evangelism. I should also clarify that when I express my opinion that evangelism is most effectively done through relationship building, I'm not speaking only of your aunt, uncle, brother, sister, husband, wife, children or parents. I'm talking about your hair dresser, your barber, the clerk you always see at the convenience store or coffee shop. I'm referring to the people you work with on a daily basis, or the neighbours that you often stop and chat with at the sidewalk in front of your house – or should. There is a harvest field at your door step. There is a crowd of people around you that, if they saw the power of God at work in your life, would cry out: "What do I have to do to be saved?" Every one of these people have questions to do with spirituality and eternity at one time or another. Every one of them will need compassion and counsel at some time during your relationship. They will lose a loved one, experience challenges in their personal relationships, or face financial struggles. Many of these people will deal with serious illness. At some time in their life they will need you to be an 'Acts' kind of Christian. You need to be in a position where God can use you when and how He wants. You need to be ready to pray with faith, believing for miracles. You need to be ready to share the love of Christ.

Today's Tools

One of the most powerful tools you have is your personal testimony. It is real. It is your life. It is easy to share because it is part of you. Your testimony speaks of the life changing power of God. People enjoy hearing about the experiences of others. It can be shared with impact because it is the story of how God impacted you. The Samaritan woman that Jesus ministered to at the well went into the village and shared her testimony. As a result "Many Samaritans from the village believed in Jesus because the woman had said, "He told me everything I ever did!" (John 4:39, NLT) Your testimony about the joys of 'God in you' is one of the most under-used tools you carry in our fruit bearing tool box.

There are various ways that you can easily prepare to present the story of God in you. To be able to confidently, succinctly, and effectively share face-to-face what God has done for you personally is extremely important. We will discuss ways to increase the effectiveness of telling your story. Realistically, however, there can be roadblocks to this. Some people completely resist any face-to-face conversation about God. This may vary with the surroundings, and who else is present. Others need to be in a place where they can reflect to take it all in. Sometimes the environment makes it difficult. The hair dresser or convenience store personnel may find it inappropriate or awkward to talk about God in their work place. It may even put their job at risk. The list of complications is numerous. So, here are a few suggestions:

- Prepare your testimony in an attractive, well written, booklet format that you can easily hand to someone at an appropriate time. Common computer software makes it easy to produce something nice and attractive. Have a copy close by at all times. Keep them in your car or in your purse.
- Record your testimony on a CD. Many people have in-house recording devices, or even studios. For a few dollars, if not free, you could have your testimony recorded. This way, people could listen to your story in the privacy of their home or car.
- Your Facebook or Instagram accounts can be great tools of evangelism. They are a venue through which the story of God in you can be shared with the world. If you design your account appropriately, it would be simple and effective to invite someone you are ministering to as a Facebook friend. These online tools are also a place where you can chat and develop relationships with people you would never have

opportunity to even meet otherwise. It is extremely important to make sure that the message these tools present is consistent and Christ honouring.

- Your church web site could have testimony pages, where you and others in the church share their stories. Most people will visit a church web site long before they will go to a church. If there is someone in your church family whose story may minister more specifically to a given individual, you can direct them to that testimony as well as your own. This also serves to begin to establish a relationship between the individual you are ministering to and a place of Christian fellowship. You can invite them to church to meet the person whose testimony they have read.
- With the technology available to us today, the means by which we can share the story of God in us is vast and varied. Let's make it work for God.

Tips for Telling

Here are a few tips for preparing the story of God in you that will increase its impact. These principles apply to every means of telling that story, whether it be face-to-face, written, or in an audible format.

- Tell a story, don't preach a sermon. You want to keep this as relational and personal as possible. Do not try to make this a high-pressure presentation of the Gospel. Write or record it as if you are casually sharing with someone in their living room.
- There are three essential components to an effective life story. They are: 1) B.C. 2) J.C. 3) A.D.
  - B.C. – Talk about what your life was like 'Before Christ'. Examine the things that motivated you through life, and where that was leading you. What significant life

experiences set you on that path? What emotions or feelings about yourself or life in general controlled your behaviour?

o J.C. – Talk about when 'Jesus Christ' came into your life. How did you come to the point of giving your life over to Him? Did you notice an immediate change in your behaviour, approach to life, or how you felt emotionally? If so, what were those changes?

o A.D. - Accepting Christ as your Saviour began the process of dying to self and living for Him. What long term impact has the decision to live for Christ made in your life 'After Death'? Relate back to your life B.C. and explain how your motivation and direction in life has changed. How has Jesus altered the impact of the former life experiences that set you on the path you were on? What emotions or feelings control your life now?

- Remember that this is not your testimony. It is God's testimony. It is the story of what God has done in and for you. Be careful to not glorify yourself or your past lifestyle. You are, of course, an integral part of the story, and what God has saved you from is an important part of that. It is of vital importance, however, to place the focus on the positive change God has made in you, and on Him as a person.
- Do not speak negatively about a church or another Christian believer, even if you have had some negative experiences in the past. This will only serve to enhance the reasons a person may have for not getting involved with a local church family, or even God.
- Be careful about using Christian jargon. Not everyone understands or can relate to terms such as "saved", "converted", or "washed in the blood". Those are important Christian terms that they will hopefully

come to understand in the future. To the un-churched, some common Christian terms may sound like religious nonsense or be completely strange to them. You don't want the terminology you use to be a reason for them to stop listening to, or reading your story.

- Have a hook. Do NOT embellish, but make your first sentence something that will grab their attention.
- Be logical. Every story has important specific elements that progress and build on each other until it reaches a climax. Each of those elements must connect in some way. Your story must be presented in a way that the listener or reader can not only follow it easily, but is anxious to hear what happens next.
- Be specific without making the story cumbersome by giving excessive facts and details.
- Be impactful. If you're old enough to talk, your life is full of events and stories. Since most people's favourite topic of conversation is them self, you have to be careful to only share the events of your life that will have the most impact on the person listening or reading. God has, no doubt, blessed you in remarkable and numerous ways. You don't have to tell them all at this point.
- Use Scripture, but use it sparingly. Again, this is a testimony, not a sermon. It is very appropriate, however, to make people aware that the Bible is your guide book for life and that its principles are life-changing. Two or three brief passages would be very appropriate.
- Be brief. If your story can't be told, read, or listened to in five minutes or less it is likely too long.
- Conclude by summarizing what your relationship with Christ means to you. Express your desire that the listener consider asking Christ into their life as well.

- Edit. Edit. Edit. Make sure that the grammar is correct. If it is in written format, use correct spelling. In representing Christ, you must be careful to do all things with the greatest possible degree of excellence.
- On the cover, label, or at the end of your text, include a means by which you can be contacted. If you are uncomfortable giving out your full name, address, or phone number, your first name and an email address would be sufficient. This allows the person to follow up with you if they have questions or comments. If they don't do so, try to make certain that you have a means of maintaining contact with them. You don't want to pressure them, but you do want to have an opportunity to ask if they've had a chance to read or listen to your testimony, and if they have any questions.

Our entire lives must be the story of God at work in us. This will be the case only when we bear the fruit of His Holy Spirit consistently. The fruit of the Holy Spirit must be the fruit of our lives when we are alone with our spouses, with our children, when we are at the work place, when we are at church, or in the world. Our lives become the story of God at work in us when we strive to be representatives of His righteousness on earth, endeavouring to be holy as He is holy. Our lives become the story of God in us when we move and minister in His anointing, revealing His power and love as the church did in the early chapters of Acts. Tell about God through your life. Then tell about God by sharing the testimony of all that He has done in your life. The world needs you. The world needs the message of Jesus Christ as Saviour. Go into all the world and bear fruit.

ABOUT THE AUTHOR

Tim has been in full time ministry since 1984. While most of those years have been in the pastorate, Tim spent five years in iterant ministry, preaching and teaching Kingdom principles that would increase the church's impact on the community. Tim has also written 'The Road to Revival', as well as a number of booklets. These are small books that tackle big biblical issues. They can be downloaded at no cost from < above-all-else.ca >